ESSE...
PSYC...
General Editor
Peter Herriot

AI

AN INTRODUCTION TO
PSYCHOLOGICAL SCIENCE

ESSENTIAL

A

B

C

D

E

F

PSYCHOLOGY

AN INTRODUCTION TO PSYCHOLOGICAL SCIENCE

Basic processes in the analysis of behaviour

David Legge

Methuen

First published 1975 by Methuen & Co Ltd
11 New Fetter Lane, London EC4P 4EE
© 1975 David Legge
Printed in Great Britain by
Richard Clay (The Chaucer Press), Ltd
Bungay, Suffolk
ISBN (hardback) 0 416 81520 0
ISBN (paperback) 0 416 81530 8

We are grateful to Grant McIntyre of Open Books Ltd. for
editorial assistance in the preparation of this Series

Contents

Preface

Twenty years ago this book would almost certainly have included the label 'experimental psychology' in the title. Historically, psychology has moved towards increasingly precise and informative methods of enquiry. The method of controlled experimentation is the most informative and reliable so far devised. However, this method is not applicable to all problems. It requires a background of knowledge before it is feasible to devise appropriate experiments. At one time the basic processes considered in this book and in this section of the series constituted the set of problems which were amenable to experimental analysis. Not surprisingly, therefore, this set of problems came to be distinguished by the label 'experimental psychology'.

As psychology has matured, experimental methods have been applied increasingly to problems that fall outside the range of basic processes. Yet 'experimental psychology' has continued to be used as a label to describe that earlier set of problems. It is clearly now a misnomer, no matter how valid a description it was in the past. I prefer to name it 'basic psychology'.

I admit readily to several beliefs about psychology. These include the demonstrable fact that behaviour is not random and in so far as it is systematically organised, it may be analysed. Furthermore, I believe that the same essential methods of enquiry that lead us to our understanding of the physical world about us are also applicable to psychological phenomena. This preconception, as is argued in the first two chapters, is not

7

blind; the data of individual experience, for example, are not denied. However, they have a limited role to play in the establishment of psychological science.

My thanks are due to all who contributed to this book no matter how unwittingly. These include the many original minds whose work is alluded to without attribution. I am especially grateful to Hilary Klee who tried to remove the worst inaccuracies and infelicities of style in the face of irrational resistance. Valerie Elliott struggled with my handwriting and made it readable in typescript.

Editor's introduction

All of us have different ideas of what psychology should be about. Those who come fresh to the subject often have expectations which are later disappointed. David Legge readily admits that many of these expectations are perfectly reasonable and often very important. It *is* important to us to be able to understand and talk about our private experience; and it is vital that whatever knowledge we have about human behaviour should be applied in humane ways. However, private experience and public service are not the topics of this book. Rather, its central concern is the scientific activity of examining behaviour in controlled conditions and drawing inferences from it about mental processes.

This book belongs to Unit A of *Essential Psychology*. What unifies the titles in this unit is the notion of the human being as a processor of information. Like a computer we can register information, code it, perform operations on the coded version, store the result, and subsequently retrieve it. Moreover, like a computer, we can use our output, or behaviour, as feedback or evidence by which to monitor our subsequent performance. The authors in Unit A are more concerned with making generalisations about people than with exploring their individual differences. Further, they deal with personal mental processes rather than with interpersonal social processes. They also probably place more stress on the traditional scientific experiment as a source of evidence than do most of the authors of the other units. However, the computer analogy may not be suitable for handling other situations, where there is no immediate sensory experience or no easily identifiable consequent behaviour. And some psychologists also feel that it detracts from the concept of the individual as a person who can consciously act upon and control his environment. The reader will find other general conceptual frameworks in other units. Psychology is struggling to do justice to the complexities of its subject matter; it is hardly likely to find any single analogy to encompass the richness of human behaviour and experience. Coming to terms with a variety of explanatory frameworks may decrease our confidence in psychology as a mature science; but perhaps it is best that we should be honest about what we don't know.

Essential Psychology as a whole is designed to reflect the changing structure and function of psychology. The authors are both academics and professionals, and their aim has been to introduce the most important concepts in their areas to beginning students. They have tried to do so clearly, but have not attempted to conceal the fact that concepts that now appear central to their work may soon be peripheral. In other words, they have presented psychology as a developing set of views of man, not as a body of received truth. Readers are not intended to study the whole series in order to 'master the basics'. Rather, since different people may wish to use different theoretical frameworks for their own purposes, the series has been designed so that each title stands on its own. But it is possible that if the reader has read no psychology before, he will enjoy individual books more if he has read the introductions (A1, B1, etc.) to the units to which they belong. Readers of the units concerned with applications of psychology (E, F) may benefit from reading all the introductions.

A word about references in the text to the work of other writers – e.g. 'Smith, 1974'. These occur where the author feels he must acknowledge (by name) an important concept or some crucial evidence. The book or article referred to will be listed in the references (which double as name index) at the back of the book. The reader is invited to consult these sources if he wishes to explore topics further. A list of general further reading is also to be found at the back of this book.

We hope you enjoy psychology.

Peter Herriot

1
Formal and informal psychology

The major stumbling block that threatens to trip up most attempts to define psychology is the combination of the literal (Greek) derivation of the word itself and the layman's expectations.

Mind-Study?
The word 'psychology' derives from the Greek words 'psyche', meaning mind or soul, and 'logos', meaning readings or study. Apparently, therefore, psychology is the study of the mind. Historically, such a conclusion would be acceptable to some but not to others. Furthermore, it would have been more acceptable before 1920 and after 1965 than during the intervening period. Psychologists' views of what psychology is about are dynamic. It is by no means certain that the views expressed today will be in tune with consensus opinion in ten years' time.

The main reasons that militate against accepting 'mind-study' as a description of psychology are twofold. First, the only mind open to direct observation is one's own – and even that may be delusory. To illustrate this problem using a mechanistic, inorganic example, one should not expect that a computer could both do sums and say exactly how it does them! It is clear that a human's behaviour is imperfectly explained by what the behaving human says about himself – even supposing that he is not seeking to mislead. He remembers a face, poem, telephone number or whatever. Very seldom can he say how. 'It just came to

not mind study

me' would be a characteristic answer to such a question. True, there are a few circumstances where one almost fails to remember, and sometimes success is achieved by deliberately, though covertly 'searching through one's mind'. These occasions are rare. Mostly we can say nothing about the processes that must be working away deep down in what some would call the preconscious or unconscious mind.

The second principal objection stems from the first one. Since direct observation of the mind of another is impossible, such an enquiry begs the question that he even has a mind to observe. Such a statement, if made about oneself or one's friends, would normally be considered insulting. However, since Darwin expounded his theory of evolution, and stressed similarities amongst species, we must ask questions more broadly than just in relation to our own species. So, are we certain that chimpanzees have 'minds'; or cats, horses, tortoises, alligators, wasps, flat-worms, hydra, paramecium or the humblest amoeba? Come to that, if a computer can be programmed to play chess at master standard, has it, when so performing, a mind?

There are a number of ready solutions to the paradoxical position one is led to through the above reasoning. One can decide categorically that mind is a property of mankind but denied the remainder of the animal kingdom. Such a view puts mind on a similar plane to soul. Alternatively, and equally radically, one could deny the existence of mind in all cases – reserving it as a description of that which one knows about and which no other person can know. Mind is then the fodder of introspection – what is seen, if anything, when one looks into oneself. Both of these extreme views have had some currency in the past. The first is implicit in a number of religious views. The second view is implicit in the behaviourist psychology of Watson (1919).

Another conception of mind exists which is less dogmatic than either of these. It is the notion that observable behaviour is dependent upon unobservable processes and mechanisms. These underlying factors both give rise to actions and to the perception of feelings and moods. Some of their activities can be 'seen' by looking inwardly upon oneself, some cannot. We have no way of knowing the proportion of the 'iceberg' which can be discerned. Nor can we know whether the 'mental' iceberg is qualitatively homogeneous. There may be something different about the part

12

we can get at. In this view mind is the total conglomeration of underlying mechanisms. The more complex the organism, the more complex these mechanisms need to be. It is not implausible to place man at the top of the mental scale since he has the richest behavioural repertoire on earth.

This view seeks to turn the question from 'mind-or-not' to 'how much mind?' In addition the critical concept of inference is introduced. Mind is not observed but implied by behaviour.

Motes and beams — *man more complex rather than superior*

I have no doubt that this attempt to replace the commonly-held belief that man is categorically superior with the less arrogant notion that he is more complex, will probably not succeed at the first attempt. Psychologists themselves may well reject this notion since their primary goal is often the study of man *per se*. It is here that resides one of the biggest problems. Logically, psychology could be concerned broadly with the study of behaviour, but, in practice, different psychologists in leaving their individual marks in the psychological literature also manifest their idiosyncratic reasons for studying the subject at all. It is not hard to see that, if a researcher is primarily concerned to study himself, his public concern for the subject may be vicarious and he may then lean strongly towards an individual, introspective orientation restricted more or less completely to human beings. At the other extreme a biologist manqué might be expected to minimise the differences between species and to seek those general characteristics that span sections of the evolutionary scale. He is unlikely to see man as closer to god than the beast of the field. And he is, perhaps, likely to be relatively more objective, less self-involved with his investigations.

Perhaps one of the biggest difficulties students of psychology have is to divorce themselves from the fact that they are members of one of the species they study, and what is more, the one species in which most of them are pre-eminently interested. In the practice of medicine it is argued that a doctor should avoid treating people with whom he is emotionally involved. It is argued that such involvement may impair his judgement. When a human studies another human psychologically he runs a similar risk. One conclusion that follows from this is that humans would be better advised to eschew the study of *homo sapiens*.

However, this counsel must fail. Many psychologists are motivated by the prospect of understanding human behaviour, though seldom do they publicly admit that they want such knowledge for their own use. Furthermore, the death-knell of a human-free psychology is tolled by the fact that imperfect and incomplete though psychology is at present, it is useful in improving the education of children, the sum total of human happiness and the quality of life.

With tangible rewards of that kind in prospect the extra difficulties of working with human subject matter must be accepted.

Everyone's a bit of a psychologist

We are veering in this discussion towards the notion that psychology is best conducted with a degree of remoteness between the investigator and the subject of the investigation. This is the state of affairs which is customary in other sciences. The nuclear physicist, bio-chemist or marine biologist does not wear his good citizen's hat when he is going about his scientific work; he does not *relate* to a proton, a molecule of ribonucleic acid or a shoal of plankton. Would the psychologist not be well advised also to separate his attitudes to man as a fellow-being from those to man as an object of scientific investigation?

One of the major forces which tend to make such a degree of objectivity difficult is the near universal tendency to generalise from oneself to others. Were it not the case that some degree of generalisation were valid social intercourse would be grisly indeed. We are more often than not right to assume that Joe today will resemble in his behaviour Joe yesterday. We can then predict how best to interact with him, for our mutual benefit. We go further and assume that certain behavioural patterns have predictive validity even in people we have never met before. If pushed to justify our predictions we would probably point to the similarity between them and people we know. We continue to do this because, provided we stay within a given cultural grouping, our predictions have a much better than chance probability of being correct. In more technical language we have, through our experience, absorbed a number of systematic relations among behaviour patterns. Though we have probably not induced formal rules from these data, we do use them for interpreting the probable implications of behaviour observed later.

14

We are, in short, acting informally as psychologists.

There is also a belief that some people are better than others at making predictions about others and at controlling other people's behaviour by means of subtle techniques. It is our experience that this is true – though social psychologists would probably say that such individuals possessed greater social skill rather than that they were better 'psychologists'. However, the exercise of such a skill depends upon an adequate basis of information and the knowledge of how far to take a generalisation before it becomes unduly risky. The judgements made by people of people in this way tend to be 'gut-reactions' – they feel right. There is seldom a reportable sequence of thought processes which precedes the establishment of an opinion and the execution of some action. Unconscious work of this kind tends to be the rule rather than the exception. Behaviour occurs but seldom leaves tracks leading back to its origins.

So is everyone a bit of a psychologist? The strict answer is yes, but a number of qualifications need to be added. Because the processes which lead even to correct judgement and precise manipulation of others' behaviour are unconscious, informal psychology of this kind does not form a body of knowledge. Thus the chances of anyone who is 'good at it' being able to teach someone else to be equally good are very poor. The skill is not systematised and so cannot be analysed, described and conveyed. To a large extent each individual has to learn from his own experience and cannot build on a body of knowledge handed down by earlier explorers. If indeed the possession of these skills is conducive of more satisfactory inter-personal relationships, then there would be unquestionable advantages to society of developing a communicable, systematic body of knowledge. It would enable a possessor to develop such skills in a less haphazard manner.

It is the goal of psychology to provide such a systematic body of knowledge, to represent the unobservable bases of 'gut-reaction' responses and 'spontaneous' action in the form of explicit rules which provide an orderly description of behaviour and, by implication, the internal states of mood and feeling which accompany it.

Many laymen coming across a particular aspect of psychological research complain that psychologists appear only to say in ridiculously long words what most people know already to be a fact of life. I contend that the bulk of psychological research should indeed be aimed at demonstrations of 'what we know already' – but that it should be attempting to go one step further. It should be formalising a picture of the underlying mechanisms so that we could train a Martian to be as skilful in interpreting human behaviour as we are ourselves. It is important to discover how we do the things that we know we can do.

So here is the distinction between the formal and informal psychologist. The latter unconsciously collects information and develops a scheme or system which allows him to respond appropriately. The former is attempting to discover just how he and others do this. The latter uses techniques of information appraisal but it is up to the former to discover just what these are. The former in turn has to appraise information and he requires a methodology to guide him. He adopts the methodology of science. It is the only one available that is likely to lead to development of the public communicable body of knowledge which is being sought.

Why bother?

Perhaps we should consider why such a public communicable body of knowledge should be sought at all. What value would it have if available?

The motive that is often said to drive the pure researcher to tackle apparently insoluble problems is 'because it's there'. The very existence of a problem is a sufficient stimulus to attempt to solve it. A similar motivation has been attributed to the rather more dangerous pursuit of mountain climbing. Alternative self-indulgent explanations are offered by suggesting that it is in the exercise of problem-solving skills that the researcher gets his rewards. It is fun to do something well. These kinds of explanation are clearly incomplete because they could apply as well to research in molecular biology, group theory or the early Plantagenet monarchy as to psychological research. Individual interest in the problem is the additional feature.

There is another kind of motive which perhaps leads more fruitfully towards an answer to the 'what for' question. Since most research has to be financially supported to make it possible, why do those organisations which supply the money choose to do so? There are broadly two levels of research, pure and applied. Applied research is distinguished by being expected to lead to more or less immediate changes. For example, in the 1950's the growing awareness of the limitations of our natural fuel resources such as coal, gas and oil led to successful attempts to harness nuclear energy. Similarly, prior to the adoption of new coins on the change-over to decimal currency in Britain, the Applied Psychology Research Unit in Cambridge was contracted to carry out a study of the suitability of coins of various shapes and size to the consumers' convenience (Wright et al., 1969).

Pure research has more nebulous aims, mainly the pushing back of the frontiers of ignorance. The benefits of the greater knowledge consequently available are usually not immediate or even immediately evident. Frequently some other change has to occur before that knowledge is exploited by application. For example, the basic principles of the computer were conceived by Babbage in 1820, but the full impact of computers had to await the development of semi-conductor technology and micro-miniaturisation of electronic components. Now the computer has become a dominant influence upon life, relieving man of many repetitive and slavish chores, which he does relatively inefficiently.

The reasons for funding applied research are explicit. A practical answer is needed to a practical question. The return on investment is potentially large and rapid. Since pure research makes no claim that it will throw up applicable results and theories, it is more difficult to understand why it should be supported. The answer is essentially one based on faith. The belief is that a solid foundation of basic knowledge will make the solution of practical problems easier and quicker. If one knows how a system works, it is easier to change it or to find remedies when it goes wrong. One can even argue that pure research is a better investment. Applied research aimed at a circumscribed problem may provide an answer to that particular problem, but unless general principles have been discovered, a new but similar problem may have to be tackled in exactly the same way. The specific solution will not generalise. For example, discovering the optimal height of seating for Post Office sorters is a soluble problem. However, unless the relations between body size, seat height and angle, nature of activity and layout of the environment have been investigated in depth, a different seating prob-

17

lem will have to be treated in the same *ad hoc* way as the first.

The benefits of pure research are potentially more distant but they can be discerned. They provide the background that makes applied research on a particular problem more efficient. Pure research is undertaken largely for its own sake; direct benefits to mankind are deferred.

From this point of view, it would be expected that the greatest need for pure research would be during the infancy of a discipline. It is at such a time that applied questions are hardest to solve. Not only is there little background knowledge to which to refer, but in the absence of an understanding of the structure of the underlying mechanisms, it may even be difficult to formulate questions in a soluble form.

Scientific responsibility

In other, older sciences the problem of what one does with scientific knowledge tends to arise after the knowledge has been acquired, and often after it has been applied. Not infrequently the question is stimulated by an abuse of knowledge. Man's experience of the unfettered application of technical discoveries has come home to roost in recent years and stimulated the various lobbies which seek to preserve the environment and to shackle the technological juggernaut. This provides a new context for discoveries, and one which preaches very great caution in the development of their application. For example, genetic engineering is likely to be a real option in ten years' time. Selective mutilation of chromosomes may make the manipulation of physical and even psychological characteristics a possibility. Even the development of clones of identical individuals may come under experimental control. Huxley's *Brave New World* has come to life in many ways already. His 'soma' has its twentieth-century alias in the form of cannabis and LSD. Many of his ideas about the technology of transportation are now feasible. However, it was his view of the social organisation of man that was the most horrifying. Biological advances suggest that it would be technically possible to produce a 'Brave New World' by the end of this century – if sufficiently powerful people wanted it.

With increasingly sophisticated technology the consequences of its misuse also increase. Consider the relative destruction

18

caused by an arrow, a shot-gun, a field howitzer and a nuclear warhead. It is because the scope of the consequences of abuse rises steeply with technological sophistication that concern over the misuse of technology has now become evident.

The main cause for concern about biological and physical technology is its impact on man. This impact is usually indirect, though no less significant for that. However, should there be correspondingly dramatic technological advances in psychology the impact would be direct and the persuasive power of immediacy gives especial significance to it.

This discussion of responsibility in science is a preface to considering further what psychology or, at least, psychologists, are about. The goal of psychological enquiry may be to understand how behaviour is organised and the factors which influence and control it. But only the most naive would imagine that finally all we should do is to sit back and admire the system in operation. It is a natural and not unrealistic fear that once understood the system would be manipulated. In real terms this means that some people could be in a position to control the behaviour of others. It is our experience that when power of this magnitude is available it will be abused at some time or other. Let us consider how far we may be from this situation.

Is there anything to worry about?
There are three levels of understanding. The consequences that follow from each level are different. The first and most primitive is the level of retrospective description. It is possible to give an orderly account of what has occurred *post hoc*. It is not possible to predict what will occur. The next level of sophistication leads to predictive description. Provided the system is simple enough and stable enough sufficient appropriate observations may be made and, once the working of the system is understood, relatively accurate predictions may be achieved. Meteorology is currently at this level of sophistication. Weather systems are so complex that they can be understood only in terms of a simplifying model of their operation. Using high speed, large capacity computers to integrate weather data from around the globe and up into the stratosphere, predictions about local weather can be made. These are statistically very much better than would be achieved by inspired guesswork, even if they are less than perfect from the point of view of the organiser of

a garden party or sports meeting.

As our understanding of the nature of a system increases further we move into the realm of explanation. Essentially this requires more detailed knowledge of the sequence of events which represents a causal relationship between one factor and another. Laws governing a relationship give way to theoretical accounts of the mechanisms which underlie that relationship. This level of understanding allows prediction, only providing that the data necessary for prediction can be integrated before they are out of date. It also offers the possibility of control. If a system is so well understood that some if not all of the factors critical for its operation can be manipulated, then it is, in principle, possible selectively to bring about particular system states.

The thought that one can be predicted is threatening. We live with an illusion of free-will, and this would necessarily be shattered if our actions could be reliably predicted by a psychological clairvoyant. However, the notion of behaviour control is far more disturbing. It is one thing to admit that one is not the arbiter of one's fate, quite another to know that someone else is. And that presupposes that the strings are pulled by a benevolent despot! Clearly it is possible to justify a fear of psychological sophistication in the hands of the unscrupulous. Can it be dispelled?

Reassurance is offered in three ways. First, psychology has a long way to go before it achieves the sophistication necessary to achieve effective behavioural control, in excess of that already practised by non-psychologists. Secondly, it is evident from our current state of knowledge that a very considerable degree of behavioural manipulation already occurs and through psychological insights we are better able to detect and react against such influences. Finally, the adoption of a code of ethics of psychological practice while falling short of perfect control of psychological skill will at least minimise abuses.

Psychologists have indeed studied many aspects of behaviour and have attempted to formalise the mechanisms that underlie them. Those aspects of psychology which are most relevant to controlling behaviour are motivation and learning. It is known, as well by animal trainers as by psychologists, that organisms will perform to achieve a desired object or treatment (a banana, trip to the cinema, £14,000 per annum or whatever) or to avoid an unattractive consequence (electric shock, 'staying-in', being sent to Coventry, loss of 'face', etc.). At one level, control of behaviour may be achieved by controlling the consequences of behaviour. In general, this technique is limited in its application since total control of this kind is seldom achieved over human beings. It would require gigantic resources to effect such control on any but the smallest scale.

The alternative and potentially more powerful method of control is to manipulate motivation. That is, to alter the goals for which an organism will strive. This can probably be done in two ways. The simplest and quickest is to introduce a new, overwhelmingly powerful physiological need. If powerful enough, the drive to satiate this need will make other motivational considerations pale into insignificance. Opiate addiction has this property. Ingesting opiate substances by any route will sooner or later change the physiological balance of the body so that it reacts violently in the absence of the opiate. The strength of this need is said to be greater than any of the naturally occurring physiological needs except perhaps for air and water.

It may also be possible to change the motivational structure of an individual by a process of relearning that actually involves a radical restructuring of attitudes, self-concept and other relatively enduring aspects of personality. There are two circumstances in which this has been attempted with some success. The unacceptable use of this technique is in 'brain washing'. In essence the initial structure of attitudes and beliefs is subjected to colossal stress while the body is physically deprived of food and sleep. In some cases these procedures are reported to result in substantial changes in personality and a malleable state that admits the imposition of new attitudes. In this way the motivational structure of the individual may also be changed. A similar goal may also be approached in the treatment of patients with very severe mental disorders, though nowadays the methods of treatment lack the barbaric quality of brain washing. Needless to say the reasons for attempting to alter the personality structure are somewhat different in these two cases. It is also noteworthy that the psychiatrist treating the patient works within an ethical code that emphasises the patient, while the interrogator works under an oath of allegiance to a political system.

Though these are two of the more dramatic ways in which attitudes, and through them behaviour, may be manipulated, subtle and continuous pressures towards change are ever present. They are either pervasive but unmanipulated pressures from the culture or the deliberate pressures applied by professional persuaders. The former are applied unwittingly by society through the agency of parents, teachers, peer groups, established institutions and so on. The latter has the deliberate aim of altering buying or voting habits for the benefit of a particular and small minority of that society. The prevalence of informal manipulations of our attitudes and behaviour is so great that either we should regard the effects of a minute number of mavericks as puny in comparison, or we should be in a state of perpetual concern lest any contact we have with any part of society change us in some way. The point is that we are always in a state of change. It is inevitable that our personality structures must reflect to some extent the social influences which impinge upon us.

In short, then, we are continuously vulnerable to informal influences intrinsic to living within a society. There are more formalised attempts to influence us but with rare exceptions these are controlled by ethical constraints in professional codes of practice. At the limit, awareness of our vulnerability coupled with our political roles offers a further means of protection.

Perhaps the most important thing to remember is that scientists have multiple social roles. They are not just boffins thrown a banana or two between equations. They are also husbands, wives, fathers, mothers, voters, teachers, and even parliamentary candidates. They have a role to play as citizens as well as specialists. They are also in perhaps the best position to detect, monitor and, if necessary, 'blow the whistle' on unethical applications of psychological knowledge. The price of freedom is eternal vigilance. Perhaps this saying has its greatest relevance in the preservation of the rights and privileges of the individual in the face of a power that threatens to overcome him. It is the responsibility of us all to protect him.

2
Psychology and self

On the search for oneself

'Know thyself,' is written on the wall of the temple at Delphos. Alexander Pope wrote 'Know then thyself ... the proper study of mankind is man'. These quotations raise the distinction between what might be called private psychology and public psychology.

To a considerable extent human judgements of others have an intuitive, emphatic basis. Implicit questions are raised: 'how would I feel in that situation?', 'what would I do next?'. When predictions are essentially generalisations from oneself, and when such generalisations are likely to lead to valid judgements, a full knowledge of oneself is likely to be exceedingly valuable.

However, it is by no means logically necessary that one should fully understand oneself before embarking on the study of others. For example, computerised medical diagnosis is made possible by establishing a pattern of contingency relations between signs, symptoms and diseases. The computer does not also need to know how it works itself.

At this point I want to distinguish between two sorts of theory; those which relate to generalities and therefore can be applied to most if not all members of the species, and those which are essentially restricted to a particular individual. The latter clearly cannot be expected to generalise across individuals. It involves essentially private theories.

Psychoanalytic theories with their postulation of complex

23

underlying mechanisms have offered a vocabulary for discussing the structure of one's own mental system. They stress the incredibly complicated issues that surround any attempt to understand 'human nature', but appear to show to each of us how some of our behaviour can be made explicable.

These and other theories about the structure of an individual's mental system are basically individual-specific. They provide a plausible set of concepts for an individual to use in identifying in himself some of the factors which influence his reactions to other people, and the external environment in general. He can use them to make sense of the otherwise confusing and conflicting information he gains from looking within himself. Part of the confusion comes from the fact that he can see only a part of the game, like a spectator at a soccer match who cannot see the ball. It is maintained here that there is no way of coming to 'see' the 'ball', with or without psychoanalysis. The argument, as before, is that a system cannot both do and know how it does. However, the game may make better sense if the balletic patterns of movement that make it up can be identified and recurring interactions defined.

As in many human endeavours it is very satisfactory to impose order on prevailing chaos. If the visible iceberg of one's mental operations can be made coherent instead of chaotic by adding a few assumptions about the hidden part of the iceberg, those assumptions will be extremely attractive. The validity of these 'explanations' is very difficult to question. In principle, any testable hypothesis about the nature of the underlying system can be wrong. However, only persisting states of organisation can be shown to be wrong. If the system is in wild and rapid change, hypotheses about transient states are likely to be false by the time they are tested. As a consequence, almost any hypothesis may have existential validity at the time of its formulation.

One of the major attractions of psychoanalytic language is that it offers a way of talking about one's own mental structure of needs and feelings. It is possible to arrive at a satisfactory orderliness using it. However, it is primarily useful because the rules of correspondence relating the data of observation to the elements of the theory are weakly specified. These weak links are thus subject to momentary redefinition and by selecting between alternative structures and using definitions that fit the current circumstances, the theory is capable of accommodating almost any change.

Two consequences follow. First, such a theory lacks predictive power. Unambiguous prediction depends upon unequivocal rules of correspondence and clearly defined relations between the postulated underlying components of mental structure. Secondly, such a theory cannot be falsified. Since the theory is available in various versions tailored to meet individual circumstances it has to be confirmed or disconfirmed in relation to a particular individual. Furthermore, the testing has to be conducted by that individual upon himself. Since the possession of any theory which helps tell a story about his mental apparatus will be better than none, and since the theory is flexible, it is no small wonder that theories of this kind tend to be personally attractive.

However, these sorts of theory are misleading. Their explanatory power is illusory since they can only act retrospectively; the future is as unpredictable as before. They are also personal rather than general in their application. The actual theory applied by a particular person to himself is idiosyncratic because the details of the theory have to be written in for his own particular case using information which is essentially private to him. Consider the philosophical problem of the nature of the colour yellow. It is in fact twofold; it is the wavelength of electro-magnetic radiation producing a given experience between green and orange in the visible spectrum. It is also the private experience produced by stimulation by that wavelength. We can determine the generality of response to a particular wavelength by asking subjects to match hues of different textures and brightnesses, and to discriminate between different hues. However, we can never determine that the inner experience of two individuals is the same. My experience of 'yellow' might correspond to your experience of 'orange'. We have learned to use the same verbal label to describe the experienced hue induced by the same physical stimulation, but there is no inevitable common path that has to be traced between the sensory input and the output behaviour of describing it as yellow.

Public and private psychologies

These considerations of the personal validity of theories leads back to an earlier distinction between psychologies. This one draws a line between public and private psychology. The latter can at best lead to a satisfactory psychology of Joe Bloggs constructed by Joe Bloggs. With good fortune it will have persisting validity so that it will be valid for future use. It might even have predictive validity in addition to offering coherent explanations of the past. However, it will not be generalisable to other individuals, because by definition the variables have idiosyncratic identities, so it would only be usable by other individuals provided the personal interpretations were contributed by that person.

Public psychologies are distinguished by their insistence on making relatively few concessions to individual variation, and those that are made relate nearly always to matters of degree rather than to qualitative distinction. They have the implicit assumption that the basic mental structure is, in terms of its external manifestations, common to the species. It admits, for example, that the detailed internal representation of a particular hue may be idiosyncratic but notes that regardless of such individual variations (if they exist!) a radiation of 600 mμ (millimicrons) produces predictably the response 'yellow' or '*jaune*' or whatever.

This insistence by public psychology on the pre-eminence of public data and the relative unimportance of individual variations on the sub-themes of the mental structure is both a strength and a weakness. Its strength comes from its possession of the scientific virtues: the power of prediction (and hence the capacity to be falsified when tested), general application to the species and possibly several species, and use of the general principles of logic as the basic calculus. It has two properties which lead to its being unpopular. First it is essentially mechanistic in form, applying the same sorts of reasoning to behaviour as have previously been used in biology and physics. Secondly, it makes few concessions to the individual vanity which makes each one of us appreciate the subtleties of our own mental structure rather more than we do those of others. Since many of us find it difficult to accept that our so special mental apparatus operates according to slavish mechanical rules, and we believe that our own individuality is pre-eminent, it is hardly surprising

26

that we tend to reject the theories of public psychology when seeking theories to apply to ourselves. At best, public psychology will do for someone else!

Provided we are aware of the distinguishing attributes and differential generalisability and predictive power of public and private psychologies, there is no reason why we should not seek both. The former has the potential to be useful to mankind in general, and to provide the basis for our interaction with others. The latter is essentially self-indulgent but may, like other forms of self-indulgence, be personally satisfying and make some contribution to establishing a healthy *modus vivendi* with ourselves. The important point is to maintain the distinction and ensure that their domains of valid application are kept separate.

It is also important to realise that the methods of inner scrutiny which are useful in the development of a private psychology of oneself are of dubious value in the construction of a public psychology that should be applicable to all individuals. The essential basis of public psychology has to be public data. These include an individual's report of his inner scrutiny or introspection but not the introspection itself. It is also quite evident that public psychology must depend upon data drawn from many individuals in contrast with the analysis of a single case that is the essence of private psychological data.

Psychological science

We have now tried to isolate several approaches to the problem of understanding behaviour. Two main dichotomies have been advanced; formal versus informal and public versus private. The distinction between formal and informal relates to the methods used in formulating and testing theories. Informal approaches are used universally and provide the bases for social intercourse but are extremely limited by the lack of codification which makes it necessary for each person to assemble his own informal psychology. One cannot build upon foundations laid by previous generations. Formal codification which leads to communication would overcome this basic limitation.

The distinction between public and private psychologies lies in both the goals and the data used to approach those goals. Private psychologies are aimed at providing an account of inner experience of a particular individual. They can only be developed by that individual (though possibly with some help

27

from outside), and they are limited in their application to that individual. Public psychologies seek to be generalisable across individuals and can therefore be constructed by one person for application to others. To achieve this goal it is obviously necessary to base theories on public data. It is also necessary to formulate theories in a communicable form.

In short then, informal psychology is the province of everyman and does indeed provide an important basis for his life. Private psychology though self-indulgent may have personal value but it has no general applicability. Formal, public psychology sets out to be generally applicable and communicable. It is based upon public data, and in seeking to establish relations amongst observables meets the usual criteria of science. The psychology that forms the content of degree studies in this country is almost exclusively formal, public psychology. It is what is otherwise known as scientific psychology. It is the study of behaviour which may lead to inferences about underlying states. Some of these may seem to have validity in terms of private experience but there is no requirement that they should do so. The goal is to develop a description of behaviour which will have predictive validity for all members of the species. In doing so it may be useful to postulate underlying states that are reportable. It will certainly be necessary to postulate underlying states that are unlikely to be reportable. Like an iceberg much of the structure is hidden to all.

3
Data, methods and measurement

Behaviour and experience as psychological data
For the last thirty years or so authors of introductory texts have tended to define psychology as the science of behaviour. Such a definition is sound and, in fact, accurate. However, at a superficial level it appears to deny the existence of experience, feelings and sentiments altogether and is rejected for so doing. But, reports of experience are forms of behaviour. They are therefore acceptable as data and provide a basis for assembling theoretical notions about the states underlying those reports. Psychology can therefore be said to be concerned with the reportable internal states, but indirectly as they are manifested through observable behaviour.

Psychology takes the Darwinian theory of evolution and derives from it an expectation that psychological functions will differ from species to species but that smaller differences will be found between closely related species. An extension of this argument would lead to the expectation that different members of the same species would differ even less. In fact, the most parsimonious starting point would be to assume that members of a given species would be identical. That is not to say that there would be no influence of differential experience but only that the basic genetically-determined structure would be common.

It is tempting to apply the same parsimony to considerations of inner experience. We should then assume that all manner of private experiences feel the same to different individuals. Yellow is yellow; pain is pain; frustration, fear, anger and happiness are the same to all.

There is only one snag about this attractively simple generalisation. It is untestable. Because these experiences are essentially private, there is no possibility of comparing mine with yours and thereby determining that they are the same or different. Therefore questions of this kind remain outside the domain of science.

It might be questioned whether there is even any point in being concerned about private experience, at least from a scientific point of view. There *is* a point, because even though hypotheses of this kind cannot be tested, that does not make them *ipso facto* false. Furthermore, if there are consistent transformation rules relating internal states to external states, useful information *may* be obtained by enquiring about internal states. For example, suppose that a pin-prick produces internal state A in subject (A) and B in subject (B) and so on. When subject (A) has internal state A present he says 'it hurts'. Subject (B), however, experiences the pin-prick when he has internal state B not state A. Similarly, neither state A nor state B corresponds to painful experience in subject (C) who needs state C to feel it. Then although the mediating internal state may differ from subject to subject there is a common and consistent relation between the pin-prick and the verbal response. If this situation holds it is quite sensible to ask any subject possessing appropriate internal mediating systems 'if it hurts'. The mapping of internal states on to responses is idiosyncratic and compensates exactly for the idiosyncratic mapping of the external stimulus on the internal states. In this way consistent responses can be obtained from different individuals even though the intervening internal states may vary from person to person.

The main purpose of the current discussion is to explore the kind of data which can be legitimately used in the study of psychology, and the inferences that may be drawn from their use. The most important criterion for data that are to be used for the development of public psychology is that the data should be public. In general this is also the essential criterion to be applied to all scientific data. That means that, in principle, each datum should be observable by more than one person.

On making inferences from behaviour

The problem of limitations on inference are less clear-cut. For example, if a subject performs a particular act, that act is not a sufficient ground for inferring that the act was intended. If he makes a mistake and calls somebody by the wrong name, it is most unlikely that he set out to do so. There are a multitude of possible roots of such behaviour. There may have been a confusion of labels; he called Joe 'Tom' because he was confident that he was called 'Tom'. Perhaps he was given false information originally. Or maybe Joe and Tom look alike and he has a persistent problem of sorting out which is which. The most obvious example would be if Joe and Tom were identical twins. Or again he may have been thinking about Tom while talking to Joe and the two trains of thought got crossed.

Clearly as soon as one seeks to probe the events which lead up to a particular piece of behaviour the alternative explanations multiply very rapidly. Some of these alternatives might be eradicated by undertaking an appropriate course of further enquiries. It would be useful to ask our subject what he could tell us about his mistake. However, we should be very cautious about taking his statements at their face value. Even though he might not be seeking to mislead us, he will not have access to all the information that we need to reach an unequivocal explanation. At best he can report something about those internal states of which he is aware. He can have no knowledge of the host of other states.

We have used the iceberg analogy on several occasions when referring to the idea that only some of the systems and processes governing behaviour are observable, even to ourselves. We know that there are a number of instances where behaviour implies prior processing of information but there is no awareness of having done so. Many complex skills such as riding a bicycle are successfully accomplished with no verbal trace of the complex integration of information and manipulation of response which logically underlies the performance. Such skills have become 'automatic', no conscious intervention is required. In fact conscious intervention may very well be catastrophic. For example, careful study of one's feet and how they should be moved while running down stairs may very well result in a trip to hospital! Presumably the time relations are upset by attempting to feed information through conscious routes instead of allowing it to be dealt with more efficiently at some lower level.

Recognition that some behaviour is dependent only upon the operation of processes that do not, or do not normally, enter consciousness leads to the possibility that even when there is a conscious correlate of behaviour, at the same time there may be an unconscious one as well. Indeed, in that case might it not be possible that the behaviour emitted is dependent on only the unconscious processes, the reportable, conscious ones being irrelevant to the actions. This possibility highlights a very important stumbling block for attempts to explain behaviour which rest mainly on subjects' reports of their private states. What they say may be true but have nothing to do with the processes governing behaviour. Returning to the iceberg analogy for a moment, this is a little like saying that we have no idea how much of the iceberg is hidden, nor can we assume that the composition of the part which is hidden corresponds in any particular way with that of the part we can observe and analyse.

In short, reports by subjects about what is going on in their heads are poor quality data because they do not have unequivocal implications. They may provide accurate information about some of the processes influencing behaviour, but they almost certainly relate to only some of these processes. There is the even more perplexing possibility that the behaviour in question is actually wholly governed by some other processes, not available to introspection, thus making whatever is reported irrelevant. We can neither vouch for the validity of these reports, nor can we argue for their universal irrelevance. At best, reports of this kind can provide another source of information. Perhaps they will be the essential stimulus for a new hypothesis about the mental structure. Such an hypothesis may be true or false but it can be shown to be neither on the basis of introspective reports alone. Tests of such hypotheses have to be conducted in the same way as tests of any other hypothesis, by the development of predictions about patterns of behaviour in conjunction with particular environmental conditions.

In this way introspective reports count as data, like any other data. On occasion they may also serve as a stimulus to theorising. They do not have *per se* the status of explanations.

How to find out

It is the essence of science to compile an aggregation of observations made coherent by a set of inferential relationships. To help such an enterprise along the way it is often valuable to erect a model (or theory) of the phenomenon under scrutiny. In one sense our mental appreciation of anything is a mental model, be it one's locality, physics or the Royal Family. In science an attempt is made to improve such models so that in so far as the parts of the models are testable they are not found wanting. This procedure can never reach the point of ultimate truth unless all parts are directly open to observation, and this is very seldom the case. In the case of psychology, one might say it is never the case.

Two main kinds of interaction between model-building (or theorising) and data collection are classically described; the inductive method and the deductive method. The former entails making unselective observations concerning the basic question and then, by a process of appreciation, inducing relationships, classifications and groupings from these data. It is claimed that the Linnaean system of botanical classification was developed in this way.

In direct contrast is the hypothetico-deductive method. This approach requires first of all some theoretical idea. Hypotheses are than devised and tested directly by making carefully selected observations. The data thus obtained are used to readjust the hypotheses and through them the original theory. In consequence of negating any hypothesis the theory is changed or extended and the process repeated.

Neither of these is a realistic description of what actually happens. Proponents of the hypothetico-deductive method are unable to say from whence the theory came, if not from some prior data. Equally the inductive approach will almost certainly involve some kind of implicit theory that determines what is observed and measured.

Psychology, like most sciences, uses both of these techniques, though never in their extreme forms. There are advantages to each. The deductive approach, most appropriate when a certain amount of knowledge has already been gained, may make headway faster. If one has specified the idea to be tested it is much easier to aim for the most relevant information needed for testing that idea. However, unless one is receptive to information that does not relate to the prevailing theory, theorising may become derivative and, ultimately, sterile, so an inductive procedure is also valuable. To some extent, radical changes in theory depend upon suspending the use of the hypothetico-deductive method.

Observation and artefacts

It is the basis of any empirical discipline that there should be developed techniques for acquiring data which are, as far as possible, undistorted by the particular technique used. It is important to be able to attribute observations to the things being observed and to avoid artefacts of the method of observation. In the so-called 'hard-sciences' like physics this problem is not substantial until one dips down into the murky depths of nuclear physics. It is not too difficult to find ways of measuring length and mass and elapsed time that are almost completely independent of the measuring instrument. Even here, however, perfection is not attained. For example, temperature variation will affect the length of the rule as well as what is measured. In addition, more subtle psychologically-based distortions may be introduced so that, in reading a measuring instrument, errors in rounding-off displayed values may be biased systematically in one direction (cf. chapter 11).

When it comes to collecting data, psychology has three major problems. These are not unique to psychology but perhaps more evident than in most other sciences. It has to determine just what characteristics of the behaviour and the situational context should be measured, to discover a way of making the measurements and ultimately to apply an appropriate analysis of the data to allow real changes to be detected against a background of random variation or 'noise'. The first problem seldom leads to a self-evident solution. More often than not the answer is implied by a particular theory. In consequence, there is a real danger that the data collected will be theory-specific. This may make such data valueless in considering other theories about the same phenomenon.

On the advantage of numeracy

Some students, attracted to psychology by its human relevance, despair of the numeracy that is demanded of them by their teachers and by the subject. At most it is asserted that real qualities are reduced irreverently to numbers, and, in so doing, the important issues are lost while the whole enterprise is made incomprehensible. A word or two in defence of quantification is in order.

Precision is one of the gods of science. It provides the basis for fine distinctions and offers the possibility of describing more exactly the relations between variables. It also provides a sounder basis for evaluating theoretical ideas, since the implications of different theories can be more clearly discerned. It may even show how apparently different theories cannot be discriminated in terms of their predictions about behaviour. One of the most compelling instances of this is described by Kintsch (1970). When the sums are done it turns out that both an all-or-none learning model and a trial-by-trial incremental learning model predict exactly the same curves for learning associations (cf. chapter 10), yet the initial gut-feeling that most students have is that these two principles should give rise to two different patterns of the course of learning. It should be added that the mathematical development of the theories also points to those aspects of behaviour about which the theories make differential predictions.

It is generally true that a mathematical interpretation of a conceptual relation is less ambiguous than its verbal counterpart. It is not inevitably the case, for it is always possible to express an equation verbally and unequivocally. However, few of us use words as precisely as we are forced to use numbers. Thus putting our arguments into a mathematical form exerts a valuable discipline on our thinking.

There are therefore two reasons for attempting to use numbers as much as possible. They are the attribute of sophisticated and informative measurement and they make our reasoning processes less equivocal. They are a most valuable tool.

Numbers are also valuable in overcoming the third problem of evaluating psychological data. Perhaps partly because of the youth of psychology, psychological measurement is normally subject to a great deal of 'noise', or random variation. For example, whereas one expects measurements of the length of a piece of string to be almost exactly the same whoever measures it and whenever it is done, behaviour, even in ostensibly the same situation, is seldom identical on different occasions. Consider a study of reading speed under different levels of illumination. One would expect variations in the number of words read per minute attributable to individual differences, the nature of the text, the colour of the print and the paper, the orientation of the text to the subject, the particular relevance of the content to the subject's idiosyncratic interests, time of day, and relation between subject and experimenter as well as the variable under investigation, lighting. In order to attribute a particular difference in performance to lighting it is necessary to eliminate the influences of all these other variables.

Inferences from data

Controlled experimentation

The reading-speed example above is a particularly easy problem. It is open to investigation using an experiment the design of which can be carefully constructed to balance out the effects of the other variables. For example, by ensuring that no systematic relation exists between the 'irrelevant' variables and the levels of lighting that we wish to study, appropriate sums can be done on the resulting data which will unambiguously focus upon the effects, if any, produced by variations in lighting. To reach unequivocal conclusions it is necessary both to design the experiment with great care and to submit the data to an appropriate statistical analysis. Fortunately a considerable number of psychological questions are open to this general approach, the essential feature of which is that the experimenter can choose what conditions should be applied to which subjects. However, this approach is not always possible, particularly when the subjects of the investigation select themselves by possession of a particular attribute. For example, consider the problem of studying the relation between smoking and lung cancer. The hypothesis is that smoking cigarettes (and perhaps any tobacco involving inhalation) for a prolonged period directly increases the chance of the smoker developing lung cancer. An experimental test of this assertion would require that non-smokers be divided into two groups, one of which would then smoke for several years while the other would not smoke at all. It would be essential that the experimenter decided who should smoke, not the subjects. Then after a period of years a count of cancer sufferers in the two groups could be compared.

Now we know (Royal College of Physicians Report, 1962) that there is a relation between smoking and cancer, in that people who choose to smoke cigarettes also tend to have a higher risk of contracting lung cancer. There is also a plausible gut-theory that prolonged inhalation of foreign bodies into delicate lung tissue is hardly likely to conduce health. However, not all smokers contract cancer and many non-smokers get it, so the association is not clear-cut. That there is a relation between smokers and cancer is undeniable; but the nature of that relation is open to question. For example, Eysenck (1963) has highlighted the equivocal nature of the evidence that it is smoking *per se* that is the culprit by offering an alternative theory. Could it not be that both smokers and cancer sufferers share a third, as yet unidentified attribute? Its possession acts both as a stimulus for developing a cancer and for the behavioural habit of smoking. One possible candidate for this factor X is 'anxiety'. This alternative view would lead to an association between smoking and cancer, but would not assert a causative relation between them. Both manifestations would be attributable independently to the hidden factor X.

Were it possible to carry out the experiment outlined above, the question could be resolved. Since the experimenter would determine who smoked and who didn't the relation between factor X and smoking would be broken and if then it was found that smokers developed cancer disproportionately often, a causative link would be indicated. From the point of view of getting an answer to the question, this experiment would be highly satisfactory. It is, however, ethically unacceptable. While one may permit others to choose to dice with death by smoking, one cannot throw the dice for them. So what can be done?

It has to be accepted at the outset that the best technique of finding out is to use controlled experimentation where all the prevailing influences are controlled by the experimenter. This technique leads to the least ambiguous and equivocal results. But it cannot always be used, either because of ethical constraints, such as those considered above, or because some factors cannot be manipulated by the experimenter. However, there are fortunately other techniques available which are at worst a lot better than nothing at all.

Correlational evidence

This little aside draws attention to another kind of technique which can provide valuable data, the method of correlation, or co-variation. The essential feature of this method is that naturally occurring variation of some particular attribute (as opposed to variation which is deliberately instigated by an experimenter) is matched up against the variation of some other attribute or attributes. On the basis that 'attributes that vary together belong together', this kind of study provides information about the nature and degree of relation between attributes. For example, back to the reading speed question, one might have found by observing students in libraries that, on the average, reading speed was related to the brightness of the lighting. The most plausible, though not the logically unique, conclusion, would be that lighting value determines reading speed directly. (The reader may like to indulge in a little cogitation and try to think of other explanations for such a correlation.)

Psychological uses of the method of correlation have been mainly in the field of individual differences. It is not possible to conduct controlled experiments entailing the manipulation of personal attributes such as aspects of personality, but it is possible to see how they interrelate in this sense. Thus, for example, it might be observed that, in general, good mathematicians are musical and vice versa. Such an observation might lead on to the hypothesis that the underlying mental structure which leads to mathematical prowess also contributes to musical skills of various kinds. It was indeed the result of prolonged use of correlational methods that led Spearman (1927) to postulate 'g', a general intelligence factor. This conclusion was based on the observation that many intellectual and academic skills are found to go together. It is only natural then to seek some single common factor which accounts for them all.

Quasi-experiments and controlled observations

There are some investigations which fall between these two kinds. They do not have the strength of total experimental control of conditions, but entail more control than the careful observational studies that lead on to statements of correlation. These 'mezzanine' studies are sometimes called quasi-experimental designs. They incorporate some of the attributes of controlled experimentation but, for one reason or another, fail to match up on all aspects.

One of the main sources of this kind of difficulty is when the attribute under investigation is a personal quality of the subject, such as an aspect of personality or a persistent feature of his behavioural repertoire. These are organismic variables. Particular instances of them cannot be divorced from the individual who manifests them. Levels of anxiety and the tobacco habit are both examples of variables of this kind. The main problem introduced by these variables is that the experimenter cannot achieve full control of his experiment, because he cannot manipulate these variables. However, even though he cannot impose a given personality upon any subject he chooses, he can set out to select subjects who exhibit particular personalities, provided he can at least measure the attribute in question. By judicious selection he can obtain groups of subjects who differ with respect to this one particular attribute. The main difference between this and a fully controlled manipulation is that the subjects 'choose' themselves. The simplest case of this sort is involved in studies of sex differences.

The main difficulties that arise from studies involving quasi-experimental designs and organismic variables relate to the generalisability of the conclusions. To what should particular observed differences be attributed? The logical impossibility of concluding that a causal relation exists between two variables from the results of a correlational study intrudes into these investigations as well.

As one becomes more familiar with experimentation and the strength and weaknesses of different kinds of design, these difficulties begin to take on more manageable proportions. In the real world it is never possible to say with absolute certainty that a causal relation exists. Some experiments and observations give better evidence and bolster up one's confidence in one causal hypothesis more than others. By attacking the same problem from many different sides the congruence of these repeated investigations is probably more persuasive than the result of a single, even repeatable, experiment of unquestionable pedigree.

4
The scope of psychology

Psychology divides into a number of identifiable parts. Psychologists are also classifiable in more or less the same way. I doubt that there now exists a psychologist capable of operating over all aspects of the discipline but there are still some who operate in more than a single one.

Orientation: processes or people
The primary and simplest division is between an analysis of behaviour which is in terms of general underlying processes and an analysis which is concerned with the behaviour of whole organisms. The former approach concedes that the whole organism may be synthesised by combination of the analytic elemental processes. But at this point in the history of psychology few psychologists wedded to this approach would reckon that they were ready to attempt such a synthesis. Likewise those concerned with the behaviour of whole organisms would agree that it often makes good sense to consider dimensions of variation between individuals in terms of elemental processes. They too would be loath to claim they were ready to offer a complete analysis.

These two different approaches are characteristic and a number of other differences stem from them. The process-oriented researcher starts with the assumption that all individuals will possess the process which concerns him: rather like the assumption that all internal combustion engines possess an inlet manifold. There will of course be individual differences but these are considered to be quantitative rather than qualitative. His research goal is to detect and describe the function of the processes which make up mental structure. Individual differences are more of an embarrassment to this aim than a phenomenon of essential interest. He doesn't have to be scratched very hard, however, to admit that none of his hypothetical processes operate in exactly the same way in different individuals. Nevertheless he anticipates that individuals are consistent and that, in principle, individual differences in the details of operation can be evaluated. He sees the priorities of his research as first to discover the processes and only secondly to give coherent accounts of how individual versions of them differ one from another.

The antithesis of this approach is that professed and manifested by the people-oriented psychologist. His primary concern is with the operation of the whole organism acting as an integrated system of processes. He may be mainly interested in those aspects of behaviour which entail interactions between individuals. His research is more closely related to every-day life and he is likely to point to such truisms as 'the whole is greater than the sum of its parts'. That is, a system composed of elements includes not only the sum of the elements but also the laws governing their interaction. His research is frequently closely related to an applied aim, if not directly so. He is clearly engaged on an enterprise which resembles what many laymen consider psychologists should be about. With all these advantages of greater 'face validity' go a number of disadvantages. Not infrequently the most fruitful way of asking an applied question is obscure. Some questions may be unanswerable within the limitations of current methodology. He is in danger of trying to accomplish a hop, skip and jump of world record proportions while not being able to do much more than sit up in his pram!

The distinction drawn here has been deliberately sharpened. Psychologists primarily engaged on holistic behavioural analyses are likely to make use of any of the findings produced by their 'process-oriented' colleagues. In fact some psychologists see the added benefits to their research of engaging in both varieties of investigation in order to crack a problem most effectively. The main reason for highlighting the distinction is in order to draw attention to the different methodologies used to study these different sorts of problems. We saw in the last chapter how different data-gathering techniques have been devised. The method of controlled experimentation, distinguished by the degree of control that the experimenter can exert over the conditions prevailing during his observations, leads to the most unequivocal data being obtained. He is able to attribute effects to agents unambiguously. Other methods to situations of greater ambiguity. In general, though not without exception, process-oriented research can be based upon controlled experimentation. People-oriented research has more severe problems. Controlled experimentation is less often possible for either procedural or ethical reasons. Furthermore, the relevant data are less likely to yield better than an interval scale metric and are therefore less informative. Thus there are real methodological distinctions associated with these two approaches.

Earlier we discussed two idealised approaches to research, the inductive and the hypothetico-deductive methods. The first of these is less demanding since although in practice some kind of theoretical context is required implicitly, it is not necessary to start with a well-defined hypothesis. The hypothetico-deductive approach needs a strong theoretical context and, optimally, the opportunity of testing hypotheses using controlled experimentation to minimise the ambiguity of attribution of observed effects. Taking these two points together it is no surprise that process-oriented research tends to be laboratory-based and seeks to apply hypothetico-deductive techniques. In contrast much people-oriented research is conducted in the 'field', the techniques are less precise and progress is generally more uncertain. There is room for more speculation and it is more difficult to eliminate inaccurate theories.

What do we do all day?

For those who seek and attain a career within psychology there is a choice of three main activities (aside from teaching). These are pure or applied research and professional practice. These categories are not mutually exclusive but serve to indicate the primary commitment of the job. We have already discussed some of the relative merits of research in chapter 1. Essentially, the only situation that can make research unnecessary is the state of perfect knowledge. We have no reason to expect ever to achieve it.

Research, however, divides as we have seen into that which is directed at a defined practical problem and that which is aimed at more distant fundamental issues. Both kinds may be concerned with 'practice problems'. For example, in order to treat clinical problems more effectively it would be as important to evaluate and improve a given treatment regimen as to conduct basic research on the essential structure of psychopathology.

There are three main areas of practice of psychology. They are specialisms that are not usually included in an undergraduate course. Typically one or two years of further study are necessary before a graduate is able to practise on the public.

These three specialisms are clinical psychology (see F3), educational psychology (see C5) and occupational psychology (see E1). The roles in society of the clinical and educational psychologists are now reasonably well defined, though that is not to say that there can not or should not be any further development. The role of the occupational psychologist is less well defined and, at present, less well appreciated by society. (Cf. B.P.S. pamphlet, *Psychology and Psychologists: a pamphlet for schools.*)

Clinical and educational psychology

The clinical psychologist is typically employed within the Health Service and attached to a hospital. Most of his work will be with patients of one kind or another. His primary role is in assessment of the psychological attributes of individuals. To help him he uses a number of psychological tests, often but not exclusively of the paper-and-pencil variety. Treatment is normally under the control of a psychiatrist, a medically qualified doctor who specialises in mental illness or incapacity. The psychiatrist usually assumes responsibility for the welfare of the patient and therefore dominates the clinical scene. The psychiatrist may however delegate a treatment role to the clinical psychologist. This treatment will be psychological rather than physical or pharmacological in form.

It is obvious that conceiving of the patient as an integrated person is even more important in the psychiatric situation than when a physical ailment is involved. Therefore it is the concern of both psychiatrist and clinical psychologist to appraise a patient as widely and as fully as possible.

Not all clinical psychologists operate in a hospital setting. For example, some are in private practice, and some work exclusively with convicted prisoners. One notable group in private practice, and who are not clinical psychologists in the true sense, are the analysts. This group includes psychoanalysts who specialise in the treatment of less severe forms of mental distress, the neuroses.

The second group of professional psychologists are also mainly employed by public authorities. Educational psychologists are usually either part of a school psychological service or of a child guidance clinic. They are specifically skilled in the dual roles of assessing educational development and promoting its improvement. In order to fulfil this role they normally have to possess considerable clinical knowledge since an accurate diagnosis of the cause of unsatisfactory progress is a necessary precursor to producing an improvement. Educational psychologists are, at present, experienced teachers as well as trained specialists. They liaise very closely with schools and other special educational establishments. Their role includes assessment but may also involve a considerable amount of remedial teaching and specialised treatment of emotional factors interfering with school progress. The boundary between clinical and educational practice is, on occasion, difficult to discern in the treatment of children. Whether the first kind of psychologist to become involved in a particular case is an educational or a clinical psychologist will often depend upon the most obvious of the presenting symptoms. If the major difficulty appears to be educational it is likely that referral to the school psychological service will be the first step. However, it may well prove to be necessary to consider a wider range of problems before the educational difficulties are straightened out. Like many categorical distinctions it is often arbitrary where one specialism begins and another ends.

Occupational psychology

The third major professional aspect of psychology is concerned with man in a work setting. The range of problems which arise here is very large and includes everything from the effects of the social organisation and communication structure of the shop-floor, office or firm to the interactive relation between an operator and his apparatus be it a capstan lathe, tower crane, or flight position indicator. Within this range is included the set of problems associated with job analysis, job design, personnel selection and training. In order to discharge all these responsibilities the occupational psychologist needs to master a correspondingly wide range of skills.

A closely associated specialism is ergonomics. This discipline is more circumscribed in its interests and includes considerations of the biomechanical and physiological factors involved in particular activities. However, there are considerable ergonomic aspects in occupational psychology (see E4) and ergonomics is itself dependent on a great deal of psychological knowledge. The main difference in emphasis relates to the specific concern of the ergonomist with equipment design and the effects of the physical environment on performance. For the purposes of this discussion I am going to treat occupational psychology and the psychological components of ergonomics together.

Occupational psychologists are engaged in all sections of the social structure. They may be employed in industry, in commerce and by government. They may play any of a multitude of roles. They are particularly likely to be found where selection and training problems are dealt with and in the design and evaluation of equipment and working conditions. The problems they handle vary from seating design and office layout and illumination to incentive payment schemes, communication structures and shift-working systems. They are also engaged on problems of rehabilitation and the design of domestic and personal equipment for the handicapped.

There is a major distinction between this professional application of psychology and the two previously discussed. Whereas clinical and educational psychologists are concerned with individual cases, the occupational psychologist is concerned with more general problems that affect sundry individuals. He must allow for the expected range of individual differences in many of his judgements but he is seldom concerned only with a particular individual.

This feature of occupational psychology means that the typical mode of operation of the practitioner also differs. The occupational psychologist will seldom be able to apply the fruits of past research and of his personal experience and training without first carrying out detailed experimental or observational

45

studies of the problem. Applied research is an essential precursor of action and much of his skill is in being able to carry out the appropriate research.

A psychological map

We have so far explored divisions of psychology along two major dimensions, activities and orientations. The relative use

Table 1 A 'map' of psychology showing the main areas of research and application and the way they divide between basic orientations towards processes or people.

| Activity | Orientation | |
	Process Orientated	People Orientated
Pure Research	Basic Psychology Physiological Psychology	Social Psychology Developmental Psychology Personality
Applied Research	Psychophysiology Ergonomics	Educational Psychology (Research) Abnormal Psychology
Application	Ergonomics Occupational Psychology	Clinical Psychology Educational Psychology Occupational Psychology

of experimental methodology has also been mentioned but it does not feature as a particularly useful basis for classification at this point. The two bases of distinction emphasised here may be used to define a 2×3 pattern of cells. Into these cells may be placed the primary groupings of interest and occupation in psychology. This classification is depicted in Table 1.

The purpose of constructing this picture is to show the primary concerns and accents of different aspects of the subject. It is not intended to suggest that the contents of different cells are independent of each other. In fact, it is shown that some areas are represented in more than one cell. Some of the relations between different areas are explored below. It is a continuing thread through this book to indicate the interrelated nature of different areas of application, fields of research and methods of enquiry. The discipline persists in its integrated form because of this essential interrelatedness. The pigeon-holes in Table 1 are not therefore to be construed as being separated by impermeable boundaries.

The row titled 'applications' includes the professional specialisms that we have discussed earlier in this chapter. The relative orientations of ergonomics towards processes and the 'helping' specialisms towards people are self-evident. Occupational psychology appears to straddle the two orientations and is concerned in part with both approaches. It is appropriate to put the applications first because they are at the interface between psychology and society in general. The other activity categories are increasingly removed from public gaze and, indeed, public evaluation and acclaim. However, they provide the essential background without which the professional practitioners would be poor indeed.

Orientations towards people

Concentrating on the people-oriented fields of enquiry, at the applied research level are found abnormal psychology and educational psychological research. Many of the individuals pursuing these topics are, when wearing other hats, practitioners of clinical or educational psychology. The research methods in these areas typically depart from the detailed examination of individual cases which characterises professional practice. Instead there is greater concern to discern general relations between variables. These researches seek to establish the guidelines for diagnosis and treatment that will provide direct benefit to the practitioner.

At the level of pure research the motivation of the enquiry is far removed from the idea of eventual application. It is essentially the struggle to solve mysteries and to extend knowledge.

There are three principal areas of enquiry here. They are social psychology, developmental psychology and the study of individual differences and personality. A section of *Essential Psychology* is devoted to each of these areas. Only a brief word of introduction will be given here.

Social psychology

Social psychology (see B1) is concerned with the phenomena of social interaction and the analysis of those factors which influence behaviour that are peculiarly derived from the relation of the behaving organism with other organisms. Problems included in this area are the formation of attitudes and how they may be changed, the analysis of communication, particularly non-verbal communication by gesture, posture and intonation, and the nature and mode of action of socially derived motivation (see D2). The majority of human actions are guided by factors other than physiological deprivation. In fact, the very existence of voluntary martyrs is evidence that on occasion social motives, such as striving for a human ideal of some kind, can overcome the apparently more fundamental physiological drive to survival.

In order to give an account of interpersonal behaviour and behaviour which depends upon reference to unseen but influential individuals, social psychologists normally have recourse to models of underlying processes that are envisaged as existing within individuals. Some of these models are based upon concepts that have been developed in other disciplines. For example, balance theories of attitude change (see B3) assume that change will occur until a state of balance or equilibrium is achieved.

It has been argued that all experiments in psychology are essentially social psychological experiments. The point here is that if an experiment involves an experimenter who conducts the experiments and a subject upon whom it is conducted, a social situation exists. In fact the implications of social psychology go further. It is assumed that the subject will cooperate in the experiment and do whatever he is instructed to do. If he does so it is presumably because he is playing to the same set of unwritten rules as the experimenter. It is quite possible to conduct experiments with greater control over the 'cooperation' of the subject. For example, since it is no good asking a white rat to perform a task, it is necessary to 'persuade' it to perform by subjecting it to some kind of behavioural control. Comparable techniques could be used in human experimentation but very seldom are. In general, it can be maintained that running any kind of psychological experiment on human subjects entails manipulating social psychological variables.

Developmental psychology

Developmental psychology (see C1) has a self-explanatory title. It is concerned with the orderly changes in psychological processes associated with increasing age, from birth (or even conception) to death, though the bulk of research has been concentrated on childhood.

The essential model for theorising in developmental psychology is a biological one. Two major influences are identified, one defined by the genetic endowment of the individual, the other the consequence of his experiences: in other words nature and nurture. It is probably senseless to assume that effects of just one of these factors could ever be observed in isolation. At a simple level the effect of an experience will be modified by the genetically determined capacity of the individual to 'benefit' from experience.

One of the many spurs to solve the riddles of developmental psychology is incorporated in the saying 'the child is father to the man'. If the nature of the adult was wholly determined by genetics then developmental psychology would become a relatively straightforward exercise in plotting the landmarks of that development. However, it is quite evident that childhood experience may modify if not totally determine profound characteristics of the adult. For example, there is evidence that the degree to which adults manifest jealousy and competitiveness depends upon the social structure in which they are reared. If the society is one which sets no store on the concept of personal property or individual prowess then the children are more likely to become cooperative and generous adults. The distinct possibility that experience in early years produces persisting effects on the adult makes a thorough knowledge of developmental psychology of unquestionable value. It may provide one means of achieving some improvement in our society.

Personality and individual differences

The psychology of individual differences (see D4) has two main facets. It is concerned with identifying the dimensions and range of individual variation. It is also concerned with identifying the idiosyncratic set of attributes which together define an individual's unique personality. The major orientation of this area is clearly towards people but a great deal of the research has attempted to make sense of individual differences in terms of particular underlying dimensions of variation which imply processes. The area divides into two main parts. One deals with abilities and particularly those which relate directly to school progress and adaptive problem solving. It would be expected that individuals at one end of this scale would be the most educable and make the greatest strides in society. At the other end are those who have severe mental handicaps and may be incapable of learning any but the simplest skills. This attribute has been called intelligence and massive efforts in the past have resulted in both theories about the nature of abilities and a number of standardised tests of ability. One major study (Spearman, 1927) proposes a general factor of intelligence modified by a number of specific subsidiary factors which relate to particular kinds of skill. For example, the brightest child at one school subject is also likely to be good at many others. However, he will be relatively better at some than others. It would be possible to account for his standing in different subjects in terms of high general intelligence and in addition high ratings in, say, mathematics and physics, and lower ratings in biology and history.

Theories of this kind are essentially descriptive but they have a predictive role. The original stimulus for the development of intelligence tests in 1911 was to find a rational basis for distinguishing those children who would benefit from 'normal' education from those who would not. Prediction of this kind can only be faultless if the sample of behaviour observed in the test is characteristic and if the individual's abilities are unchanging. Neither assumption is likely to be wholly true. We are constantly changing and changing most rapidly during the time we receive schooling. Inevitably, even with the most perfect test conceivable, a proportion of predictions must be wrong.

Although, for these practical educational-policy reasons, studies of intelligence have been an important component of research into individual differences, the problem of understanding the non-intellectual bases of individual differences is, in principle, greater. These are basically the enduring, characteristic features of his emotions and motivations. They define to a large extent the interests he has, the things he values and influence the particular life-style he adopts. One of the simplest of the attempts to provide an orderly account of these features seeks to characterise each individual by placing them at a point in a space defined by two axes. These are extraversion/introversion and neuroticism. In theory any particular individual can be defined by two numbers, one on each axis. A number of different questionnaire tests claim to assess a person's location on these two dimensions.

One of the positive advantages of this kind of theory is that it incorporates the notion that in most instances mental disorders can be seen as extensions or extrapolations of normal personality. Such a view is not only in contrast with much older views of demonaic possession but it offers an optimistic approach to treatment in terms of adjustment instead of radical interference.

Orientations towards processes

The applications of psychology which are process-oriented have already been discussed. They are principally the ergonomic aspects of occupational psychology. It has already been argued that this application is distinguished from others by the generality of its operation. As a consequence of its separation from a primary concern for particular individuals, it is feasible to conduct experiments in order to arrive at the optimal arrangements of men, machines and the working environment. In this way research is inextricably entwined with application.

Psychophysiology

There is another kind of applied research which can also be labelled process-oriented even though its application is typically in a people-oriented area. This is psychophysiology (see A2).

In the next chapter the relation between psychological processes and the matter that mediates 'mind' will be considered more fully. For now it is sufficient to assume that behaviour implies a physical system. There are good reasons for inferring that the head is the part of the body which houses most of the processes underlying behaviour. Therefore it is natural to consider the physical system composed of nerve cells to be the prime seat of behaviour.

These considerations lead to the view that neurophysiology may well give some valuable pointers to psychology. In fact, one of the most valuable contributions of physiology is to provide additional indices of function which complement behavioural measures. These indices are threefold. They include recordings of brain activity either by observing single neurons or by looking at brain waves more generally, measures of neurophysiological function based upon chemical analyses, and peripheral indices, mainly of the electrical activity of the skin.

Perhaps the most intensive application of psychophysiological research is in the field of abnormal psychology. Many abnormal psychological conditions (i.e. psychopathologies) also manifest different patterns of psychophysiological behaviour. The physiological measures may then be helpful in aiming at a meaningful classification of the disorder. They may also open a window on brain function and give some clues to the origin of the behavioural disorder. Ultimately this line of research might be expected to lead to a rational basis of physical treatments. Perhaps this relation between behaviour and physiology can be illustrated by considering a motor car that has broken down. Operation of the controls does not produce the normal and desired changes in its 'behaviour'. The psychologist is in the position only of observing the manipulation of the controls (input) and the consequent behaviour (output). He cannot lift the bonnet and conduct the kind of fault-finding by selective examination of the components of the system that a garage mechanic would. However, the majority of cars provide a number of additional indices of the system's performance. For example there may be an ammeter indicating the performance of the electrical charging system, a fuel gauge, an oil pressure gauge and so on. Intelligent inference from this supplementary information may lead to an accurate diagnosis of malfunction. To be specific, loss of power in conjunction with a very high temperature of the water-cooling system may indicate a corroded or jammed thermostat. Having made a precise diagnosis of this kind, the remedy is relatively easy – remove or replace the thermostat.

Human beings are rather more complex than motor cars,

and, so far, psychophysiology does not yet provide sufficiently unequivocal supplementary information to enable man to be mended as efficiently as his motor car. However, the status of psychophysiology in relation to psychology is comparable with that of the supplementary displays on the instrument panel. Psychophysiological indices give that additional look at the works that may ultimately lead to a more precise understanding of its function.

The psychological ivory tower

Ivory towers are notable for rising above the hurly-burly of everyday life to give peaceful, pressure-free working conditions for their inmates. Universities have long been designated ivory towers because of a belief that the work going on inside them is hardly at all relevant to the needs and activities of society outside. The only justification for this taunt is that universities do provide sanctuary for pure research. Problems may be studied there without being continuously influenced by the demands for answers to practical questions. There is therefore an opportunity to work up the background of understanding of basic processes that is an essential foundation for handling practical problems efficiently.

The derogatory implication of 'ivory tower' cannot be justifiably applied to the varieties of psychology so far discussed. The professional application of psychology may be imperfect but it is hardly irrelevant. Likewise applied psychological research is so named because of its direct relationship to practical problems. In a slightly different way people-oriented pure research is unlikely to attract censure since its manifest concern with human beings as individual organisms points to its eventual usefulness.

One section of psychology, however, is in danger of being singled out as a self-indulgent pastime akin to solving crosswords or playing cats'-cradles: that is process-oriented pure research. It is this section which stands at the greatest distance away from practical relevance in the real world. As we have already seen, the justification for pure research is the expectation that eventually, by understanding the fundamental processes underlying behaviour, practical problems will become more easily soluble. There is, of course, no necessity for each individual researcher to subscribe to this 'hope of the science' (and of the Research Councils!). Individual scientists may indeed pursue their own interests for much the same diverting reasons that they do crossword puzzles.

Pure research tends to have two distinct stimuli. The first is theoretical, the second is derivative from practical problems. An example may aid this classification. Consider the general problem of learning. Since the problem is complex it is necessary to begin by advancing relatively simple theories and developing from them. One such simple notion is that learning entails the formation of associative links between internal representations of stimuli and responses. This is a kind of telephone-exchange model. It may be postulated further that these associations are formed in an all-or-none manner (Guthrie, 1935). It turns out that this theory is extremely difficult to test. Forty years later it is still not possible to give a categorical answer. Ultimately, research on the problem of learning may give rise to knowledge that will influence education and training; in the meantime it is necessary to derive some satisfaction from attaining lesser goals.

The applied stimulus for pure research tends to be found in areas where there is a manifest lack of background information. Consider a problem about the design of a radar display for air traffic control purposes. One of the problems air traffic controllers have to be continually aware of is the possibility of a collision. In order to reduce the probability of such an event, aeroplanes are constrained to fly at different heights and with considerable lateral separation. A difficulty arises, however, either when pilots fail to obey their instructions, or when two planes at the same altitude fly on converging courses. One task of the air traffic controller is to identify potential collision courses. Two difficulties in doing this are promoted by the apparatus. The sweep of the heavens is represented on a small screen entailing a massive reduction of scale. As a consequence the spots representing aircraft move very slowly. Secondly, the display is discontinuous, being revised each time the radar scan rotates. Between each scan the display fades. These two factors combined make it difficult to discern the course being flown by the aircraft, and hence complicate the task of detecting impending collisions. The design problem is how to improve the display in order to make the controller's task easier, and, by so doing, improve his performance.

It turns out that very little is known about the perception of the direction of movement, and even less about the process that enables perceived movement to be spatially extrapolated. Thus in order to discover what characteristics of the display will produce the greatest effects on performance, it is first necessary to conduct a considerable amount of pure research into the basic perceptual processes underlying that performance.

In this survey of the scope of psychology there are two major areas left to mention. One is concerned with the discovery of the nature of the processes and mechanisms which underlie behaviour. These might be called basic processes, though it is necessary to repeat the caution in the preface that basic social processes and basic developmental processes are not included. The other is concerned with the physiological correlates of behaviour and experience; the 'hardware' which underlies behaviour. No satisfactory separation between these two areas occurs naturally, but an arbitrary distinction between a psychological and a physiological approach is useful, at least for purposes of explication. The relation between physiology and behaviour is the subject of the next chapter.

Basic psychology
There is a problem in finding a label for this section of the book since there is a problem in finding a label to describe the set of enquiries to which it refers. A substantial part, if not the major part, of psychology is to do with basic underlying psychological processes. The sorts of questions that fall into this category are, for example, about the input of information, how the organism 'knows' about the world outside it, how its behaviour changes, how it manipulates its physical relation to the world, and the processes governing its choice of action. These processes can be argued to be basic in two senses. They are necessary for the existence of any more complex forms of behaviour and they are apparently elemental. They would be part of the essential specification for a design of a synthetic organism.

The label that has been used in the past to refer to the study of basic underlying processes is experimental psychology. We have already, in the preface, argued against the use of this term today on the grounds that experimental methods have been increasingly applied to problems that fall outside the range of basic processes. These extended problems include, for example, processes that are specific to social interactions and psychological development, and many others. So the term 'experimental psychology' has no longer a clear definition and leads to confusion. Texts such as Woodworth and Schlosberg's *Experimental Psychology* (1938, 1954), Osgood's *Method and Theory in Experimental Psychology* (1953) and Stevens' *Handbook of Experimental Psychology* (1951) reflect this confusion of content and method. There is no point in perpetuating the use of a methodological label to imply a certain content when that content is changing all the time.

The simplest alternative is the term 'basic psychology'. This term is directly concerned with content rather than methodology. It is not free from criticism, but seems the best available, short of inventing a new word – and psychology has enough potentially confusing technical terms already.

The content of basic psychology is the subject of this unit of *Essential Psychology*, and is introduced in this volume in chapters 6 to 10 inclusive.

Physiological psychology
Psychophysiology has already been discussed as a special area of process-oriented applied research. It was characterised as a source of independent information about the functioning of the system. Psychophysiological data can complement behavioural data and thereby augment the sum total of information available about the brain-behaviour system.

Physiological psychology is a related area but its goals are slightly different. Essentially it is concerned to identify the physiological processes that subserve particular psychological processes. In principle, one would anticipate a reciprocal relation between physiology and psychology. A knowledge of the relevant physiology could indicate what kinds of processes are feasible, a knowledge of psychology may suggest what kinds of physiological processes should be sought. The relation between physiology and psychology is examined in chapter 5.

5
Hardware and software

Minds and bodies

This chapter is concerned with the relationship between psychological variables and the 'stuff' upon which they depend. It is essentially the 'body-mind' problem in modern dress.

Classical approaches to body and mind made no clear distinction between them. However, since Descartes, considerations of their relationship have started from the apparently self-evident assumption that they are separate and distinct. This starting point then leads naturally to a consideration of how they interact and theories about the influence of each on the other. This view stems mainly from an implicit definition of mind as internal experience and having much in common with an insubstantial but independent soul.

More recent views conceive of experience, behaviour and physical states, such as those that come under the scrutiny of the psychophysiologist, as facets of the same system. Thus behaviour and experience are indices of a particular state of the total system. The system itself consists of material substance describable in terms of biochemistry, physiology and anatomy. The working of the system may be manifested either through behaviour or by changes in detectable physiological or biochemical indices. The phenomenon of experience indicates that the capability for self-reference is one of the attributes of the system.

At the present time our knowledge of the organisation of behaviour and of the structure and function of the underlying physiology is inadequate. Neither is sufficiently well understood to provide a strong foundation for precise theories about the relationship between them. The evidence that there is a relationship, however, is beyond dispute. One of the properties of living matter is 'irritability', the capacity to respond to stimulation. In fact the diagnosis of death hinges on the concept of permanent cessation of this capacity. Equally it is inconceivable that behaviour can exist in the absence of matter. Even inanimate forces such as gravity are the product of 'stuff'.

Reductionism: '. . . lesser fleas upon their backs to bite 'em'
Having accepted the idea that psychological variables are a manifestation of a physical system, it is an obvious question to ask if it would not be more sensible to examine the physical system directly. In fact, this is an argument for giving an account of behaviour in terms of physiological or biochemical variables.

For example, consider a behavioural act such as signing one's name. A signature is generally accepted as a kind of psychological fingerprint. Consider again how this act could be described. The psychological description, at a molar level, would be that 'he signed his name'. One could go a stage further, down to a more molecular level, and describe the temporal pattern of muscular contractions which produced that signature. This would be a physiological description. Another, more central physiological description would be in terms of the brain activity which leads to the muscular activity. One might consider an even more minute analysis in terms of the biochemical changes involved and describe the release of molecules of transmitter substances that make the 'connection' between one nerve cell and the next in the chain; and the movement of electrically charged ions across cell membranes. Though these analyses have never been done, there is no reason, in principle, why they should not eventually be possible. Possible or not would they be worthwhile? Would the resulting account of a signature be better in some way?

The reductionist viewpoint is that one gets closer to the ultimate 'truth' by seeking even more minute units of analysis and by reducing them to descriptions of physical events wherever possible. Such an approach requires one to follow the course from psychology to biochemistry.

There are two reasons why such a course may lack the revelational properties hoped for. First, it is clear that the complexity of a description increases as the size of the elemental units of that description decrease. Coding information in the largest chunk that is possible without obscuring important details is obviously economical. Economical codes will be more efficient for communication either between individuals or in the internal manipulation of an 'idea' within one's own mind. For most purposes the concept 'signature' is unambiguous and informative and more easily 'handled' than a lengthy description of muscle twitches including their relation one to another and their organisation in time.

The second argument against a reductionist description is the problem of alias. A signature can be written with either hand, the feet, the mouth or with those mechanical arms which are used for handling radio-active substances behind a lead protective barrier. These different versions of signature would probably differ markedly, and possibly not all would be recognisable as coming from the same agent. However, one can also sign with many different writing instruments, of different weights and size and held in different grips. These different signatures are likely to retain whatever is the essential discriminating feature of a personal signature. However, even though all are recognisably and distinctively Blogg's signature, the pattern of muscular activity giving rise to each must be very different. Just consider differences between signing with chalk on a blackboard, and signing a cheque with a ball-point. In the former case the movement mainly involves the wrist, elbow and shoulder, in the latter the essential squiggles are due to finger flexion and extension. We must conclude, therefore, that the defining feature of the signature cannot be attributed to particular muscle movements *but rather to a pattern that is to some extent, independent of the motor system which is involved.* This alias problem makes a physiological description even more complex and a biochemical description inconceivably complicated. Even if possible, it is no surprise that one should ask what is the point.

This discussion highlights the concept of level of description or explanation. If a detailed analysis of underlying mechanisms is required, it is unavoidable and, no matter how daunting, physiological mechanisms and processes may have to be invoked. However, a satisfactory description at a more molar, large scale level may suffice and, if it does, it will be superior in terms of economy of handling.

Given that there may be reasons like these for preferring a shorter, psychological account to a longer, more detailed physiological one, why bother with any explanations at non-psychological levels? The answer is that they may help, for, on occasion, there is an obvious relationship between underlying psychological mechanisms or processes and physiology. Knowledge about one has immediate implications for the other. Finally, a complete account of a behaving system must include an account of the structure and operation of its physical components. If only functions were specified there would be no way of distinguishing it from a suitably programmed computer.

Balance of payments

Like the natural sciences, once called natural philosophy, and, far enough back in time distinguished neither from each other nor from philosophy itself, psychology was spawned by philosophy and philosophers. Centuries later psychologists were frequently given 'house-room' in university departments of philosophy before they achieved departmental independence. However, the empirical foundation of psychology has driven a wedge between these two subjects and other experimental sciences have become more welcome bedfellows. The first fruitful attempts to measure sensation came from a physicist. The first time that an elemental aspect of learning was captured, it was by Pavlov in a physiological laboratory. Even more recently, it is ideas from communications engineering and acoustics that jolt the imagination of psychologists. The philosophical landlord has long been supplanted as the 'onlie begetter' and prime influence in psychological advancement.

The early investigations of the senses by Weber and Fechner were linked with what was known or could be discovered about sensory physiology. The strategy seems to have been the straightforward one of studying structure and function as alternative faces of the same coin. Quite early, however, the nature of the trading relation became clear and it was evident that an equitable balance of trade was unlikely. In essence this arises because even the simplest piece of human behaviour entails the operation of brain processes most of which remain a total mystery.

Certain bits of physiological information point to particular psychological questions. For example, the division of much brain tissue into right and left halves, invites questions about dual representation or localisation of function (that is, the responsibility of certain areas of the brain for certain sorts of behaviour). Although many questions about brain function are of mainly physiological interest some may have great psychological importance. For example, information to be processed must enter the central nervous system through one of a very limited number of routes. These routes do not necessarily lead to both hemispheres of the brain, at least not in the first instance. Images cast on the right side of the retina by objects on the left side of the viewer give rise to nerve signals which arrive only on the right side of the brain. If these stimuli are linguistic symbols they will be dealt with more slowly if presented to the right cerebral hemisphere than to the left, since linguistic analyses seem to be preferentially conducted in the left hemisphere. This is a clear instance in which knowledge of the underlying physiology makes sense of otherwise confusing psychological data.

One of the most exciting recent discoveries in sensory physiology was that of Hubel and Wiesel (1962). They showed that particular cells in the visual cerebral cortex (in the occipital lobe at the back of the head) respond specifically to elongated shapes in particular orientations. Others respond only to movements in particular directions. These findings had special impact because they bore on the theoretical suppositions of behavioural researches such as Sutherland (1964) who, in order to make sense of discrimination behaviour (see A3), proposed that the visual system is so organised that shapes and movements are coded by analysis in special ways. Hubel and Wiesel's complex cells offered a physiological identity for Sutherland's analysers. Here is an example where the plausibility of a hypothetical psychological process is greatly increased by finding a physiological structure that could mediate its function.

Earlier attempts to find physiological or anatomical correlates of behaviour tended to concentrate on the relation between brain structure and psychological function. So Gall (1810) sought to identify particular areas of the brain with certain psychological 'faculties' and proposed that skull 'bumps' reflected the development of a local part of the brain and of the corresponding faculty. This early attempt at establishing localisation of function has become more sophisticated and now involves direct investigation of brain activity using electrodes. It has also become clear that the more important relation is between behaviour and patterns of activity in the brain rather than just their locations.

It is probably because the psychological level of coding is easier to communicate than the physiological that psychology can contribute to physiological research. The complexity of brain function is such that it is hard to decide what to look at next. The existence of particular psychological phenomena may offer guidance. For example, behavioural evidence implies that the organism varies in its sensitivity to stimulation, and in the degree to which it attends selectively to particular forms of stimulation. Physiologists observed that stimulation applied to part of the base of the brain (in the brain-stem) caused an increase in the activity in the higher centres of the brain (cerebral cortex) usually assumed to be responsible for complex (and conscious) behaviour. This brain-stem structure, called the reticular formation after its net-like composition, was found to receive information from the sensory apparatus in parallel with the main input routes ascending to the cortex. It was clearly a first-class candidate for the function of awakening the cortex to deal with the incoming information. The discovery of centrifugal fibres descending from the cortex to the reticular system indicated an even richer property since it offered, in principle, the capacity for the cortex to control its own input. A mechanism for selective input had been identified which might form the physiological basis for the psychological phenomenon of attention.

These arguments emphasise the essential relationship between brain and behaviour, that makes imperative an appreciation of psychology by brain physiologists and of neurology by psychologists. Each discipline has a major contribution to make to the other.

Model-building

This discussion might appear to demand that processes postulated as underlying behaviour be conceived of in physiologically identifiable terms. No doubt, such an identity would be highly desirable for the neuro-physiologist. However, neither psychology nor neuro-physiology are ready to proceed in that way. Most attempts at model-building (theory building) are in terms of hypothetical processes and mechanisms which have no overt identity in the language of the other discipline. This is particularly true of psychology which finds it valuable to postulate such underlying variables as expectancy, association, strategy, dissonance, and need for achievement. The value of these concepts is that their use results in testable hypotheses being formed.

In fact, psychologists anticipate that an adequate codification of behaviour should be achieved without recourse to explanations in physiological terms. Furthermore, they expect such accounts of behaviour to be achieved before a physiological explanation is possible. Thus it is not surprising that the great majority of psychological theories make no explicit reference to the underlying 'stuff' which is implicitly supposed to mediate them.

It is a modern fashion to refer to relatively specific theories about circumscribed aspects of behaviour as 'models'. There is a perfectly good reason for doing so, but it could apply equally to the corresponding activity in physics or marine ecology. Essentially the scientist is faced with a more or less chaotic set of relationships between observable and, hopefully, quantifiable variables. He seeks to render these relationships more meaningful by finding some super-ordinate pattern which imposes some structure on the chaos and which accounts derivatively for them. Consider observations of the heavenly bodies. The ones that do not twinkle, the sun and the planets, move in an orderly, though complex, fashion. The classical, Ptolemaic, view took the model of the earth as stationary and sought to discover the rules governing the movement around it of the other bodies in the solar system. A much simpler model was suggested by Copernicus and Galileo who proposed the sun as the centre of the system. Even then the development of this helio-centric theory by Kepler was inordinately complex until Newton established the laws of gravitation which finally brought a description of planetary motion down to manageable proportions.

These developments are marked by steps that can be characterised by postulating 'what if it works like this?' questions. A structure or set of relationships is matched up to the data and, if it fits, accepted as providing a way of establishing orderliness in the data. Often these ideas for organisation are taken from outside the realm of the observations. For example, Lorenz' model of the relation between the release of certain fixed-action-patterns of instinctive behaviour in animals and the presence of specific stimuli may be likened to a lavatory-cistern. It flushes when the lever is operated. If the cistern is over-full only a slight pressure is required. It may, if unflushed for some time, even start to flush spontaneously. Extraordinarily, the cistern model also serves for the operation of single nerve cells!

Models tend to be either or both of two kinds. The first kind of model is one in which the functional operations are a property of a physical system. The second type of model is simply a statement of the functional operation in abstract terms. The latter type of model is usually stated in mathematical terms and the function embodied in it is therefore usually stated very precisely. The former type of model may specify the functional operation only intrinsically by reference to a particular physical system (such as a lavatory cistern) and lack an explicit statement of the system's operation. This kind of model is an analogue model.

Models have played a very substantial part in the development of our knowledge about psychology, as they have in other sciences as well. Psychology has enjoyed certain advantages over other sciences by virtue of its more recent birth. In particular, ideas developed in physics, biology, mathematics and statistics have been available as the bases of models for psychology.

The impact of computers

Man has been described as the only large capacity general purpose computer that can be produced by unskilled labour. This definition goes a long way to showing how the development of large and powerful computer systems has so influenced the thinking of some psychologists as to lead to computers being used as models of man.

Certainly there are many things that man has in common with these powerful machines. Both take in information, process and manipulate it and alter their outputs in consequence. Even the simplest logical operation by a computer exemplifies this, but a more impressive demonstration is to program a computer to play chess or some other rule-governed game. There have been many demonstrations of this kind, the most persuasive, perhaps, being those in which the computer learns to play the game better by playing with more skilful human opponents.

It comes as no surprise to learn that with successes of this kind in simulating behaviour, it has been proposed that a greater understanding of psychological processes might be acquired by finding out how to produce successful simulations.

There are, of course, definite limitations to the conclusions that may be drawn from such simulation studies. Computers work in particular ways. They are bound by a logic determined by their construction. Most general purpose computers are based on binary (two-state) logic since electronic circuits capable of an all-or-none response, that is of being either active or not, are simple to produce and reliable in operation.

Two-state logic appears to be reflected in the operation of the nervous system since neurones either 'fire' and transmit an action potential from one end of the nerve cell, or they do not. The analogy may end there, however, since different nerves manifest action potentials of different magnitudes and the electrical potential of a nerve cell both before and after the synapse (the gap between two nerve cells) is a graduated rather than an all-or-none variable. Nonetheless the binary nature of nerve activity has promoted the analogy between brain action and the way computers work.

Hardware and software

The operation of a computer is completely determined by two influences. These are the way it is built and the instructions it has been given. These are functionally identical constraints, but one is due to its physical structure and therefore a persistent feature of the machine. The other is due to the loading of its memories with carefully chosen information which guides the way in which it works. This is the program and is infinitely flexible. The physical system of constraints is known as hardware, the program which guides its operation is known, in contrast, as software. When a computer is in action, its operation will be a joint function of hardware and software. Particular features of its operation can be attributed uniquely to one factor or the other. For example, whether it displays information through a teletype or on a screen will depend upon which facility it possesses. If it possesses both then it will normally be software which determines which output route will be active.

65

This distinction leads to a fairly obvious analogue model of behaviour. It is postulated that some behaviour, or some aspects of behaviour are determined by the structure of the brain. This, in turn, is determined by the genetic blue-print that guides its development. Behaviour which is of this kind could be described as innate, or 'wired-in'. It is hardware determined. Much insect behaviour, though astonishingly complex, is probably largely of this kind. In contrast, most behaviour of human beings seems to be a product of learning and experience. Experience may be thought of as a program which governs the operation of the hardware. The accumulation of these 'programs' over the years of infancy, childhood and adolescence leaves the adult in possession of a vast library of programs.

The language of computers and information-processing machines can be used in the analysis of behaviour, and, in particular, in describing hypothetical systems that could provide models of behaviour. It offers a different way of thinking that has been demonstrated to be useful in the domain of machines, and therefore is not an implausible candidate as a language for psychology.

That said, it would be a mistake to suppose that the analogy between man and machine can be drawn tight. There are a multitude of differences in behaviour which counsel caution. Perhaps the most outstanding is the difference in the laying down and retrieving of information from memory. The computer can retrieve any information stored within it, provided that the key to unlock the appropriate memory is available. In this sense it has perfect recall. The human is somewhat more fallible. Details of events, easily recalled soon after their occurrence, are no longer retrievable weeks later, even though the general features of the event are remembered. On the other hand, the human can provide his own retrieval 'keys' and is not bound by the present stimulus. The human also has astonishing capacities to extract information, to digest information, abstract essentials and to determine that he lacks information. These capacities far outstrip those which currently we can coax from a machine.

The most obvious difference between machines that process information and man who may operate in a similar way, is emotion. Machines do not 'blow their tops' in the face of frustration, they just output a cool message such as 'error in data'. It is this, perhaps, which most distinguishes them from biological systems. And for this reason, if for no other, a computer-based model of man will never be completely satisfactory.

Behavioural contexts

The message of this chapter is that psychology has some important relatives. Perhaps the two most important ones at present are neuro-physiology and computer science. The former by describing the nature of the stuff of the behaving system adds to the overall picture of that system and can, in principle, limit the range of hypotheses made about its underlying structure. The latter is concerned with the structure and function of large inorganic machines that are capable of a behavioural repertoire not too dissimilar from that of the organisms psychologists study. Both through the use of simulation and the development of analogue models, computers may help in the development of theories of the operation of complex systems and, eventually, through them, human behaviour.

6
Routes of knowledge

A behaving system is dynamic. It is in a perpetual state of change. It takes in information about the world, transforms that information, imposes goals of its own, responds to thwarting of its goals, seeks information and alters its surrounding context. Living material is spontaneously active.

In seeking to describe the processes which make up such a system an arbitrary decision has to be made as to where to begin. There is no simple linear progression through the system that makes more logical sense than any other. It would be as defensible to start by considering the goals for which it strives, the way in which it adapts to circumstances and acquires new ways of responding, or the systems that integrate information. Nevertheless, this story is going to begin by considering the processes which provide the system with knowledge about itself and about the world around it.

Exteroceptors

Different species possess different powers of sensitivity to physical stimuli. There are two main sources of such stimuli. One is inside the organism, the other outside. External sources provide information which leads to a definition of the environmental context of the organism and its place within it.

Organisms of a relatively simple kind possess the ability to respond to direct forms of stimulation such as physical force, temperature, dampness and sundry chemical substances. The membrane defining the outermost layer of the organism (and preventing it from diffusing into its surrounding environment) may be uniformly sensitive to these forms of stimulation.

Further up the evolutionary scale a wider range of physical stimuli may be sensed, including a narrow band of frequencies on the spectrum of electro-magnetic radiation – that which is known as light. Sensitivity to physical force also increases so that rapid changes in pressure may be discriminated, giving rise to the sense of hearing. Man possesses the capacity to sense light, sound, sustained pressure, temperature and a variety of chemical substances. He has specially developed apparatus such as the eyes to sense light, ears to sense sound, skin which mediates touch and temperature, olfactory and gustatory apparatus to mediate smell and taste respectively.

All these senses are receptive to stimuli which impinge upon the organism from the outside and therefore imply something about the world in which it exists. Some of the senses require direct contact, others are said to act at a distance. In fact the distance quality of distance receptors is an inference made by the brain.

The ultimate in distance senses is perhaps that sense that responds to gravitational force and other accelerations. This is the vestibular sense. The apparatus which subserves it is housed inside the head near the innermost part of the hearing apparatus. It consists essentially of a number of spheres in a viscous fluid. This apparatus is, in effect, a set of accelerometers disposed to respond to both linear and rotational accelerations. They respond regardless of the source of the acceleration, thus they cannot discriminate between the acceleration due to gravity and that due to an increase in velocity in the horizontal plane. It is because they combine naturally that leaning over on a bicycle when taking a corner at speed feels no different from cycling in a straight line. The vestibular sense then both signals information about externally imposed forces like gravity as well as internally generated accelerations like rotating the head about any axis.

Interoceptors

Although most people are aware of the importance of exteroceptors because they tell us about the outside world and our relation to it, the integrity of the system probably depends just as much on the sensory apparatus which conveys information about the system itself.

It is useful to distinguish between the parts of the system which process information (that is mainly the brain and spinal cord) and the remaining parts which may be considered to play an essential but subsidiary role. The system has to be fuelled, metabolic products have to be conveyed and waste ejected. The system has to maintain its structural form and has specialised systems interfacing it with its environment. At one side (the input side) of the system are the exteroceptors, at the other (the output side) are the various means available for altering its location in the environment and for manipulating the environment itself. The role of the interoceptors is to tell the brain what is happening in these subsidiary parts of the total system.

The two main groups of interoceptors are chemoreceptors and pressure-sensitive receptors. The former come in a large number of different forms specifically sensitive to a narrow range of stimuli. There are receptors for oxygen, carbon dioxide, blood glucose and a host of other substances. They play a vital role in maintaining the vegetative systems of the body and providing information to the control centres in the brain and spinal cord.

Pressure receptors are varied in form and also in their relation to other structures. In slightly different forms they are found in the joints, in capsules in tendons connecting muscles to anchor-points and in other regions such as the gut. They are also found in the highly specialised muscle spindles, which probably provide the 'master' part of a master-slave servo-control system for muscles, similar to the power-brake and power-steering systems fitted to motor-cars.

A combination of the information provided by the joint-receptors and the tendon-receptors, coupled with some of the information from the vestibular system, provides proprioception. This is the sense by which the system knows how the various bits of it are positioned in relation to other bits of it, and how they are moving. It is this sense that tells you where your limbs are when you have your eyes shut. It is an essential source of information for the performance of most perceptual-motor skills ranging from picking up a glass of beer to playing badminton on ice.

There is a third segment of interoception which is still something of a mystery. This is pain. It was once thought that there were special nerve endings, so-called 'free' nerve endings because they were apparently not specially structured, which mediated the pain sensation. However, discovery that some areas of skin have nothing but free nerve endings led to revision of this simple notion. It seems that any stimulus that causes damage to the innervated structure is sufficient to produce pain, regardless of whether the damage is caused by heat, caustic chemicals or physical injury. One theory asserts that the pain stimulus is just very severe stimulation of the mechanisms that otherwise convey different senses such as touch and the temperature sense.

Sensory inferences

We tend to take for granted the idea that we are separable from the world about us. It seems self-evident that things are happening in that world. A train passes in the distance, somebody calls to someone else. A cat celebrates yet another success. However, the brain knows nothing except that it receives signals from a variety of different nerve fibres. It has to integrate these signals and interpret them.

The way in which the brain can be fooled may be demonstrated (on oneself) by closing both eyes and gently tapping one eyelid. It works best if one taps one side of the eyeball. If done optimally there will be several sensations including touch (if not pain) and flashes of light. These are caused by physical stimulation of the photo-receptors which normally respond to light. They are much more sensitive to light stimulation than to being knocked about, but when they respond, no matter how stimulated, they respond in the same way. It seems that if signals reach the brain from these receptors, the brain interprets them as evidence of light. The brain has no way of knowing that it is being fooled.

All perception has this property. The brain receives information about the state of the sensory apparatus. It has to interpret this information. It does so in the way which is most parsimonious. The sum total of one's sensory experience makes it simpler to infer a physical world outside our skins than any other explanation.

In the last chapter it was asserted that science progresses by offering models of systems up for comparison against data. This *modus operandi* is itself a model of how the brain works when faced with incoming information. It has to develop a model and

71

test it against the incoming information, adjusting the model until the data are congruent with it (see A4).

An example of this is provided by the Ames distorting room. This is a room shaped like that shown in Figure 1.

Fig. 1 *The Ames distorting room*

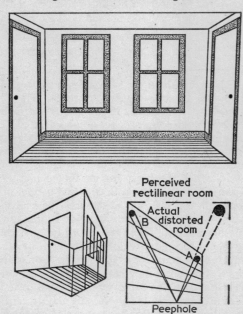

Perceived
rectilinear room

Actual
distorted
room

B

A

Peephole

Above is shown what a subject sees with one eye. Below is a perspective drawing and a plan view of the room. The right-hand wall is a rectangle but the back wall and left-hand wall are not. The left-hand door is much larger than the right-hand door, similarly for the windows. The floor slopes downward from right to left.

The room is not rectangular but the dimensions have been calculated so that at one point of viewing it casts an image on the retina of the eye which is the same as that which a rectangular room would cast.

If now two identical objects are placed at points A and B in

72

the room, A will appear very much larger than B. Even more dramatic is to have a room large enough for a person to walk about in. If, viewing him from the same point, a stooge walks from A to B, he will be 'seen' to change size. This latter effect will not be so strong if the subject (the viewer) knows the stooge extremely well (such as a spouse) but is very strong if the stooge is a stranger.

These effects can be accounted for by deducing that the

Fig. 2 *Set of three ambiguous figures*

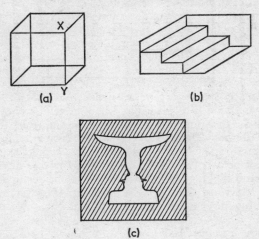

(a) Necker cube: the vertical line XY may be seen as either a front or back edge.
(b) Schröder staircase: this staircase goes either up or down.
(c) Rubin vase: vase or lovers in silhouette.

brain, used to experiencing rectangular rooms, perceives the room as rectangular. After all there are no cues available about its real shape. The distortions of the size of objects then follow, given the retinal image they throw coupled with the incorrect assumption about the room shape. The brain can be persuaded to make some adjustment to its 'rectangular model'. For example, if the subject explores the room tactually, using a long stick, the illusion diminishes. Presumably the reduced effect found when the subject is emotionally involved with the stooge is the result of the brain being more prepared to adjust its assumptions about the room than about the wife.

There are numerous other examples of the brain's model-building propensities. Psychologists have devised a number of ambiguous figures such as those in Figure 2.

The essential attribute of these figures is that there are at least two ways of seeing them. For example, the vase can also be seen as two faces looking into each other's eyes, the Schroeder staircase can go either up or down, and the Necker cube can also take either of two distinct orientations.

The fascinating feature of these sorts of figures is not that the brain is getting identical information and has two ways of organising it, but rather that only one of the alternative models is available at a given instant. There may be relatively rapid alternation of the alternatives but they are never contemporaneous. Another important fact is that even though the brain has one apparently satisfactory model it does not stick to it if another organisation is as plausible. Many viewers seeing such a figure for the first time, and unaware of the ambiguity, may see only one alternative for several seconds, or even a minute or so. But suddenly and without any warning the first, apparently stable percept will vanish and be replaced by the alternative. The sophisticated observer can, to some extent, manipulate the effect and increase the rate of alternation. However, even he cannot 'refuse' ever to see the alternative.

Maintaining a stable visual world

Except under the influence of drugs, when very tired or perhaps after being submitted to some bizarre fairground apparatus, we take a stable visual world for granted. It behaves lawfully. Domestic cats stay the same size as we approach them, they do not expand into lords of the jungle. The world tends to stay where it is, it does not gyrate as we look around it. We should beware of failing to wonder at the amazing processes that are necessary to bring about such stability.

Consider first the stationary world. Many have experienced the common illusion of misattributing movement. If one is sitting in a train, looking out of the window at another train close by, it is often difficult to know which train is moving when one pulls out. Usually the situation is disambiguated by further information, either obtained by looking out of the other side of one's train, or by noticing the vibration, or lack of it. This problem is caused by the fact that the movement of the retinal image of the train outside is the same regardless of which train moves. The brain needs additional information to choose an unequivocal model of the world.

This same basic problem exists when one moves one's eyes or one's head, and views a moving scene. Is the scene moving or is oneself moving, or both? It turns out that this is not normally a difficult problem to solve. A very elegant system of compensation exists. The brain takes a copy of the instructions it sends to its various mobile appendages including the eyeballs. These instructions are called the efferent signal. If the world is stationary the efferent signal will produce a change in the retinal image. This is called the re-afferent signal. If the eyes are stationary but the world is moving the resultant retinal change produces an afferent signal. The elegant compensation which keeps the world stable is possible because the brain has a way of predicting the re-afferent signal which would result from implementation of the efferent signal. Information coming from the retinae is then corrected for the expected re-afference and any remaining movement is attributed to the world outside. In short, self-produced movement is attributed to the system, any other movement to an agent outside the system. What is more, all this takes place without a trace which is available to experience and conscious report.

A somewhat different problem exists to maintain the identity of objects in space regardless of their orientation, distance or illumination. A coin at an angle still looks circular; people do not become dramatically smaller as they walk away; blackboards still look black in strong white light. These phenomena of maintained identity are known as the visual constancies. It appears that they also are the result of the operation of some very subtle compensatory processes. The main method of investigation has been to study subjects' ability to produce constancy judgements under conditions where ancillary information is progressively withdrawn. In this way it may be shown that subjects are not able to make size constancy judgements if there are no cues to the distance of the object being judged. Similarly shape constancy depends upon information about the slope of the object. Brightness and colour constancies depend upon ancillary information about the light that illuminates the object. It should be added, before one gets too blasé about these processes, that although information necessary for the compensatory adjustment is now fairly well understood, it is not known exactly how the compensation mechanism works.

This eulogy to perceptual processes should not be allowed to go so far as to suggest the system is perfect. It is quite capable

Fig. 3 *Set of four optico-geometric illusions*

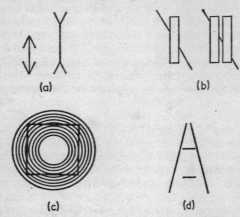

(a) Müller-Lyer: the shafts of the arrows are the same length.
(b) Poggendorf: the diagonals are interrupted straight lines.
(c) Woodworth: this is similar to the Hering illusion: the square is true.
(d) Ponzo: otherwise called the 'railway track' illusion, the two short lines are the same length.

of making mistakes. One kind of mistake is that exemplified by the optico-geometric illusions. Some examples of these figures are shown in Figure 3. All illusions of this type involve distortions of perception of the real world. These distortions are induced by particular features of the context. For example, the illusory inequality of the shafts in the Müller-Lyer illusion is due to the presence of the arrow-heads. The 'distorted' square would look as it really is, a common square, were it not for the concentric circles upon which it is super-imposed.

76

Explanations for these visual illusions have been sought for many decades. They have probably not yet been found. However, an exciting coalescence of the processes which bring about constancy judgements with these illusions has been offered by Gregory. In essence his theory is that the visual illusions occur because a constancy mechanism has been inappropriately applied. The illusions are typically found in two-dimensional drawings. Gregory argues that the brain strains to 'see' them as three-dimensional objects. It operates constancy scaling mechanisms as if the drawings were three-dimensional objects, and the illusory experience naturally follows. It is worth remembering that man is the product of thousands of years of evolution, and perspective drawing was not invented until about the fourteenth century. It would be no surprise that as a result of natural selection man possessed equipment for handling a three-dimensional world rather than a two-dimensional representation of it.

Percepts without stimulation

Perception is outstanding amongst the psychological processes because the vivid detailed quality of the percept encourages us to ask questions about it of the perceiver. No other process offers such a rich feast of introspective data. The reportable thought processes in problem solving are pale in comparison and the vague outlines of experiential emotion barely lead to articulated descriptions. It is this vividness which leads one to suppose that there must be a referent, a real tangible object responsible for it.

The geometrical illusions are one example of how all may not be as it seems. There are other, more striking dislocations of perceptual experience from reality. Dreams are a common example of this. Rarer but far more dramatic are hallucinations.

Hallucinations are perceptual experiences so strong that the hallucinator will usually refuse to accept them for what they are. To him, they are percepts and the objects seen or heard are really there. The only way to shake his confidence is to provide evidence as vivid as his hallucination but which is incompatible with it. They are not a normal phenomenon. That is, hallucinations tend to be concomitants of abnormal physiological states. They may be characteristic signs of mental disorder or associated with states of extreme deprivation such as hunger, thirst or lack of sleep. Hallucinations have also been reported relatively frequently by subjects taking part in sensory deprivation experiments. These are experiments in which subjects are placed in an environment which is made as unstimulating as possible. One technique has been to blindfold and earplug the subjects and then suspend them in a tank of water maintained at blood temperature. This treatment quickly leads to disorientation and often hallucinations of various kinds. It has been suggested that the brain, starved of information, invents some in order to maintain a target level of activity.

Dreams also have vividness and even though their content is clearly bizarre, they have immense credibility for the dreamer. The sense of relief which is felt on regaining consciousness and firmly gripping the reality of the bedclothes with both hands, is hard to forget. The credibility of dream experience is extraordinary. Hallucinations may be weird (such as the classical pink elephants associated with *delirium tremens*), but they usually obey most of the rules of normal percepts. Dreams normally incorporate massive distortions of space and time and more often than not logic is suspended. So, presumably, are the normal corrective and checking systems that must operate when awake and which exclude 'impossible' or unlikely interpretations when modelling the world on the basis of received information.

Images are, for most people, pale and ill-defined in comparison with a live percept. However, there are considerable individual differences and there are also differences in the vividness of images evoked in different sensory modalities. Galton, for example, distinguished individuals whose visual imagery was dominant (visiles) from others reporting stronger auditory imagery (audiles).

Some individuals are reported to have extremely vivid images. These images are usually visual and so strong and stable that they can be inspected in much the same way as a currently perceived scene. This phenomenon is called eidetic imagery, and is said to be more common in children. It is of very great interest, but so rare that very little experimental investigation of it has yet been accomplished.

Stimulation without percepts

Generalising from some aspects of one's own experience, it is easy to form the expectation that perception leads to a conscious reportable experience, the percept. However, it is clearly not the case that all incoming information has this effect. It may even be the case that only a relatively minor fraction does so.

There are myriads of pieces of information that must have been processed but leave no conscious trace. Most of the time one is not aware of the disposition of one's limbs but unless the brain were handling proprioceptive information about them, skilled movements would be impossible. One certainly has no awareness of baro-receptor signals, the blood-glucose monitoring system or one's blood oxygen tension, yet these are under continuous surveillance. Furthermore, finely organised corrective responses are being put into effect. If they were not, for example, and the corrections to the peripheral resistance to blood flow were neglected, sitting or standing up would cause one's blood to descend rapidly to one's boots and loss of consciousness would unerringly follow.

We are in no position to make any statements about the experiential nature of perception in non-verbal animals. However, it is clear that all except the lowliest species process incoming information in a sophisticated fashion. We do not demand that conscious experience be an attribute of perception.

7
Input to output

Behaviour, by definition, is observable. However, it is logically a product of some unobservable processes which can be plausibly divided into three different groups; input processes, translation processes and output processes. A great deal of psychological activity involves all three and some activities to be considered here seem to entail a simple progression of involvement of these processes. There is then a real sense in which information is put through the system. This chapter is concerned with behaviour of this kind, which is essentially reactive and can be conceived of as a simulation of the more important aspects of much skilled behaviour. Ball-games and car-driving are everyday examples of tasks of this kind.

From a psychological point of view one can seek to establish the relationship between input and output. This may be described in terms of the underlying processes which contribute to it and the rules which govern their operation. As compared with other more complex and lengthy varieties of behaviour, these simpler kinds of information processing would appear to have three attractive features. They are logically fundamental, they may be expected to follow relatively simple rules and, in consequence, they pose soluble problems to the psychologist.

They are also attractive problems from another point of view. The proportion of real behaviour which is of this kind is immense. Most of our behaviour leads neither to emotional involvement to a sufficient degree for us to be aware of it, nor to extended self-interrogation of internal states such as those involved in solving difficult problems. Most behaviour involves acquiring information and modulating responses so that certain goals, which change from time to time, are achieved. When reasonably skilled, we can do this 'automatically'. That is, the solutions in terms of choice of, or change of, response arise without a prolonged period of problem solving.

Perhaps the most generally meaningful example of this is driving a car. At first the learner has enormous difficulties in manipulating the controls. He may have to attend quite deliberately to the position of the gear-lever, the distance of the clutch pedal above the floor-board, and the effect of each small rotation of the steering-wheel. As his skill improves he finds that he changes gear without deliberately enacting a ritual and in steering, his concentration migrates from the steering-wheel to the direction of movement of the vehicle. He masters the still more complex relation between road speed, steering-wheel deflection and radius of turn, so that, once again, the set of co-ordinated responses necessary to make the car go in a particular desired direction emerges 'automatically'.

In this context, of course, 'automatic' does not imply that the brain of the driver is irrelevant. It implies that the behaviour is a product of brain function which does not invade 'consciousness' to any marked extent. In fact, if such behaviour is deliberately submitted to conscious analysis it may very easily be disorganised. Once again, I advise you not to concentrate too hard on what your feet are doing as you run down stairs. The coordination of responses is accomplished efficiently by an unconscious process and if conscious processes are imposed it seems that the resulting duplication of control leads to a potentially painful if not fatal breakdown of skill. These considerations lead to the interesting hypothesis that conscious processes are involved when the system has to deal with a problem that is difficult for it, either because it lacks the necessary skills or because the problem is intrinsically difficult (see chapter 8 and A6).

Input processes
In chapter 6 a number of aspects of information input were introduced. However, at that time no attempt was made to consider the nature of the functions relating physical states to which the receptors could respond, to the psychological correlates of

those responses. There are two basic problems, sensory sensitivity and sensory scaling. Both these problems are subsumed under the title 'psychophysics' and were among the first problems that were submitted to experimental investigation in the first half of the nineteenth century.

There are two aspects to the problem of sensitivity. One concerns the limitations of the range of physical stimuli to which the receptor system is sensitive, the other relates to the power of stimulation necessary to produce a response. The point was made in the last chapter that receptors may respond to a wide variety of forms of stimulation but that they are preferentially sensitive to particular forms. For example, the photo-sensitive cells of the retina at the back of the eye also respond to pressure if it is sufficiently intense.

Physically, light is a very small band of wavelengths of electro-magnetic radiation. The visible spectrum lies between about 380 (violet and 750 mμ (red) and is bounded by ultra-violet and infra-red bands. There are differences between individuals' ranges of sensitivity. One kind of red-green colour blindness is due to a shortening of the spectrum caused by non-functioning of red-sensitive receptors. There are also species differences. It is thought that bees can respond to ultra-violet 'light' that is beyond the range of human sensitivity. In general, the range of stimulation that the visual system responds to is determined by the nature of the photo-receptors which transduce the light energy into first a chemical change and through it to nervous activity.

A similar question can be asked of the other modalities. The auditory system has been investigated intensively. Hearing is due to the ear responding to variations in pressure which produce distortions in the cochlear, the specialised apparatus in the inner ear. These pressure waves may be mediated by air, water or other fluid media, and also by bone. The reason that our voices sound different on a tape-recorder compared with when we are speaking, is because the latter includes sounds conveyed by the bones of the head direct from the speaking apparatus to the internal mechanisms of the ears. A child can hear sound ranging in frequency from about 15 Herz to about 18 kiloHerz. With increasing age this range becomes attenuated so that the top end of the audible range may stop at between 10 to 12 kiloHerz. Again there are species differences. Dogs, bats and moths all have the capacity to respond to tones well above 20 kiloHerz. Bats use very high frequency sounds as the basis of an echo-location navigation system (similar to Asdic which was used for detecting objects underwater, such as submarines). The Galton whistle produces tones within the audible range of dogs but above that of humans, therefore providing a means of calling one's dog without shattering the peace of one's fellow humans.

Minimal effective stimulation

It has already been established that receptors are not sensitive only to particular forms of physical stimulation, but rather their sensitivity is preferential. Towards the end of this preferred range the receptor becomes increasingly insensitive, but there is no sharp cut-off. There are also variations in sensitivity within the preferred range. These variations are basically in the power of stimulation needed to be effective.

For over a century the concept of threshold held sway as the feature that best described sensory sensitivity. The concept is represented in physics and also has valid application to the mode of operation of individual nerve cells. It is the simple idea that if sufficient energy impinges on it the system will respond and if not, it will not. The transition is sudden and, at any given moment, the level of this stimulation which is just sufficient takes a precise value. Threshold theory has now given way to a more complicated decision theory which seeks to describe the operation of the whole system. Essentially this new theory, signal detection theory (SDT), argues that at the levels of stimulation which give rise to observable changes of behaviour, a threshold does not exist. Instead there is continuous variation in the level of receptor activity signalled to the brain. The brain is then in the position of having to decide whether the activity reaching it is evidence of a real stimulus or whether it is simply random activity which is a continuous background feature of the system's operation. It appears to make this decision by the application of a rule which leads to the binary decision that there is something present or there is not. The rule varies with circumstances, so that the criterion for responding 'yes' is lower if a signal is likely or highly valued than if a signal is unlikely or if the penalty for 'crying wolf' is high.

An important consequence of the development of this theory

is that sensory sensitivity can be measured and separated off from other factors which influence behaviour by acting directly to bias the response in a particular direction. The theory stresses the complex dependency of as simple a function as the detection of weak signals, on the operation of the whole system. It emphasises that even here the behavioural context is important and concepts such as statistical expectancy and value cannot be left out of consideration.

Psychophysical scaling

The other major question about input relations concerns the functions which describe the mapping of physical stimulation onto its psychological counterpart. For example, a linear mapping function means that for every unit increment in physical stimulation there will be a unit increment to its psychological concomitant. Investigating the nature of these functions poses some especially difficult problems. At the outset they appear insoluble, since there is no way of getting inside the organism to spy directly on the psychological dimension. Therefore indirect, inferential methods have to be used. Several techniques have been devised to study this question. All depend upon relating subjects' behaviour to level of stimulation and attributing the form of the observed function to the sensory system.

The classical answer to this question was incorporated in the Weber–Fechner Law. Weber showed that the change in stimulus power necessary for a change to be detected, varied lawfully with the absolute value of stimulation. A small change in a weak stimulus is as detectable as a larger change in a more powerful one. In fact the ratio of change to absolute value for a just noticeable difference is a constant. This ratio is called the Weber fraction. Fechner then derived from this, by adding a few assumptions, that the relationship between the physical and the psychological scales was logarithmic. The essential assumption turns out to be that, subjectively, a just noticeable difference is of a constant size. Unfortunately, attempts to test this assumption find it wanting.

A considerable encouragement to research in this area was given by the discovery that direct methods of estimation of magnitude could be used. The most commonly used method of this kind is that of magnitude estimation in which subjects are instructed to assign numbers to describe the apparent magnitude

84

of the presented stimulus. A large number of different intensity scales have been found to have a standard form of relationship. The psychological dimension is a linear function of the physical dimension raised to some power. For this reason it is known as a Power Law. The most convenient way of expressing this function is to plot the logarithm of the subject's magnitude estimates against the logarithm of the stimulus presented. A straight line results, with a slope which reflects the power to which the physical stimulus is raised. It turns out that the slopes of these plots (that is, the power functions) vary among different physical dimensions but are consistent for each particular dimension. It is worth remarking that some dimensions have been found for which an increasingly *small* increment is required to produce a just noticeable difference as the level of stimulation is raised. For example, this is the case for electric shock stimulation. The survival value of such a relationship is obvious.

Selecting among inputs

At any one moment the sensory system is bombarded with stimulation. A host of different physical stimuli impinge upon the exteroceptors and it is matched by that which stimulates the interoceptors. If all this information were to be received into the processing system, a gigantic capacity to process information would be required. Though the brain is large (comprising about a thousand million nerve cells with an even larger number of interconnections between them), it is inconceivable that all the information instantaneously available could be processed. The alternatives are either to sample momentary stimulation on a random basis, or to select some kind of information at the expense of others. The brain opts for the latter solution.

To a limited extent the system can do several things at once. For example, there is more or less continuous monitoring of peripheral blood pressure and postural change results in co-ordinated variations in peripheral blood flow to maintain cerebral blood pressure at optimal levels. It is also possible to walk along the road while having a conversation. However, there is little evidence that the brain can handle two complex streams of information at once, and none at all if the information comes through the same sensory channel. A selective mechanism operates to determine which of the competing inputs shall be accepted for processing.

The nature of the processes which bring about selective attention are as yet poorly understood. In general terms it can be said that information which has especial relevance to the ongoing activity will be preferentially attended to, as will information which has novelty value, or which relates directly to the well-being of the system, such as a threat. However, these attributes of attention raise a particularly difficult problem. How does the system know that such high priority information is available for processing without processing it? The answer seems to lie in the notion of levels of processing. Some preliminary analysis is necessary to detect the existence of information which is unpredictably present.

An example of the operation of the attentional system may illustrate this problem. It is quite possible to conceive of riding a bicycle on a quiet road while carrying out mental calculations of some kind. However, should the stability of the bicycle be seriously threatened by an uneven road surface or the sudden approach of another vehicle, the mental calculations will be shunted out of consciousness while the whole attention is given to the matter of keeping one's balance. The relative importance of $E = MC^2$ and scarred knees comes out unambiguously on the side of physical survival.

There is some evidence that the physiological mechanisms that mediate such an attentional system may, in some instances, involve a peripheral 'gate'. For example, activity in a cat's auditory input pathways can be affected by what it is looking at. If the cat is looking at a captive mouse the auditory activity is lower than if no such tasty morsel were in the visual field. This suggests that when the cat is attending intently to a visual stimulus it does not hear sounds because the brain actually turns down the sensitivity of the hearing apparatus outside the brain. However, it seems safe to assume that the cat does not become functionally deaf. The barking of a nearby dog would almost certainly be detected. There must therefore be a system for analysing the auditory input in some preliminary way, thus allowing a particularly important auditory stimulus to capture the cat's attention. The parallel input pathway system via the reticular formation in the brainstem could be the basis for such a system. The common belief that important messages get through to a sleeping subject (like mothers hearing their babies cry) appears to mirror the penetration of emotionally-toned stimuli in the distracted subject.

Mechanisms of motor control

The organisation of the response control systems that represent the output interface with the world is poorly understood. It seems that in the history of psychology those topics which are associated with conscious, reportable internal processes have taken priority. Thus a very considerable volume of research has been conducted in the field of perception, thinking and problem solving. Studies of emotion have also been popular. However, investigations of the final stages in the chain between input and output have had a Cinderella-like existence. Psychologists have been almost wholly unconcerned about leaving their organisms paralysed for want of a viable output system.

As for the input system, psychology has turned to physiology for an initial source of inspiration about the processes underlying response control. Analysis of the anatomy of motor nerves, muscles and, in particular, the spinal cord reveals that only limited advances can be made by considering the output system in isolation. There is a close integration between proprioceptive input and output control. A moment's thought reveals why this has to be so.

The motor system comprises muscles which alter the position of the various parts of the articulated skeleton. Arms are bent, fingers flexed and heads turned. Muscles contract in response to signals reaching them from motor nerves. However, the mechanical efficiency of a muscle-joint combination will vary according to the physical rules of leverage and angles of applied force, as well as the more subtle variations in muscle power with the length of the muscle. In other words, the force developed by a muscle depends upon the angle of the joint it affects. Without information about joint-angle the brain has no way of calculating the message to send to the muscle. The only other way to produce given forces or movements would be for the muscle to cease activity when a specified goal has been achieved. No doubt there are some occasions when this latter procedure is used but it leads to indecisive 'hunting' responses that are the antithesis of skill. Except in very young children, movement control is normally smooth and accurate and must depend upon sophisticated prediction of what motor signal will be required to effect the intended change in output.

Most real movements, as opposed to simple ones evoked for laboratory study, involve coordinated responses patterned in both space and time. Some of these are controlled at spinal level. The new-born baby possesses a full set of reflexes which represent basic units of organisation subject to higher control from the brain. The extensor and crossed-extensor reflexes provide the basic coordination of extension and flexion that is required for walking. A newborn baby, if supported, can be persuaded to produce leg movements that closely resemble those used in walking. As the brain matures and takes control of these peripheral centres of organisation, this reflexive behaviour disappears and does not reappear until the onset of crawling behaviour. Research on the nature of the mechanisms at brain level which subserve motor control systems is only just beginning.

Translation processes

Two main methods of investigating behaviour, in which output is linked to input by relatively straightforward rules, have been developed for laboratory analysis. These emphasise on one hand the response of the system to an isolated and distinct signal and on the other the way the system can respond to a continuously varying signal. They reflect the methods of analysis an engineer would apply in order to establish the characteristics of an engineering system, be it a radio or a vehicle suspension system. These two methods are called reaction time tasks and tracking tasks. In a reaction time experiment the subject is instructed to respond in a particular way (by depressing or releasing a key, for example) when a particular signal occurs. The experimenter records the nature of his response and its latency, that is the time elapsing between onset of the stimulus and onset of the response. Nearly all this time is taken up by the operation of processes in the brain.

Tracking entails the subject responding to a continuously varying signal so that it is necessary for him to produce the right response at the right time. The nature of the response is usually more complex than in a reaction-time task since a graduated matching of response to input-signal is normally demanded. In this kind of task the demand is not so much for a response to be made as quickly as possible, but for an optimal response to be effected that is coordinated with other events, spatially and temporally. Steering a vehicle is an example of tracking.

Both these tasks define a class of behaviour which is tightly bound by relatively simple rules. For example, in a reaction-time task a subject may be instructed to respond with the left-hand key when the right-hand light is lit and correspondingly when the left-hand light is lit. In a tracking task he may be required to keep two pointers aligned so that he has to reflect in the movement of the pointer he can control, the movement of the one he cannot control. Time is an important measured characteristic in both tasks and is used as a basis for inferring the mechanisms and processes underlying behaviour. Reaction-time tasks are more appropriate for investigating the processes involved when a subject has to choose between specifiable alternative responses; tracking tasks are more useful for enquiring into the operation of the coordination of responses. Both types of task offer information about the way in which the system responds to continuous demands since a series of reaction-time signals may be presented one after another and the distinction between the two tasks then becomes somewhat hazy.

Tasks of this kind are the main ones used in the analysis of skilled behaviour. By carefully constructing a task it is possible to concentrate upon particular aspects of the response control system. For example, a reaction time task may be varied by manipulating the discriminability of the signals to which the subject responds, the complexity of rules relating signals to responses, or the precision of the response that the subject is required to make.

One of the longest standing questions that have been asked using a reaction-time paradigm (method of experimental enquiry) is the way in which response latency changes with the range of choice of response. It is found that subjects take less time to choose between a small number of alternatives than between a larger number. The exact nature of this function implies something of the operation of the choice mechanisms. Provided the number of alternatives is relatively small, say less than fifteen, then it seems that these responses are available to subjects as pre-prepared alternatives. However, the search through this set, prior to selecting the response to be made, is neither random nor systematically exhaustive. Instead it seems that a system of selection is adopted which leads to the elimination of about half the number of alternatives on successive choices. Finally a unique pre-prepared response remains. To some extent this mode of operation reflects that of electronic information-processing systems and the application of information theory has provided psychologists with a valuable source of ideas about how the organismic information-processing system might work.

Clearly it is possible also to use reaction-time tasks as a basis for studying choice behaviour of many kinds. Until the choice problem becomes very difficult, error rate is low and so it is particularly informative to examine the speed with which choices can be made. The main independent variables (factors manipulated by the experimenter) in such experiments are the information provided to the subject and the rules relating input to output. Often these rules are not explicit. Instead a criterion is specified and the subject has to discover a response which meets it. For example he may be required to find a word which will produce a meaningful completion of a sentence. By careful design of the task the experimenter can emphasise the differential involvement of information registration and integration processes, the operation of internal mapping or translation rules, or the processes which draw up the specification of a desired response and implement it.

Cybernetics – the final cause in modern dress

The four modes of explanation advanced by Aristotle include the so-called 'final cause'. Essentially this means, when applied to behaviour, that one account of a system's behaviour may be given in terms of what it is for. This is a teleological mode of explanation since it is the outcome which is used to explain the processes which lead to it. It appears to entail a reversal of the time stream which in our experience seems to proceed unidirectionally from past to future.

For many years psychological theories disagreed about the involvement of the future in explanations of the past. For example, the choice made by a rat in a T-maze could be described either in terms of stimuli 'pushing' it one way or the other, or in terms of goals 'pulling' it. A substantial body of literature in the 1930's is taken up by the conflict between these two extreme theoretical positions. Some of the major theoretical views were S–R theories that conceived of behaviour as the consequence of implicit or explicit stimuli producing responses according to the

90

rules of association. The major alternatives were S–S theories that characterised behaviour as being dependent upon a set of relationships between perceived events (stimuli) which provide the basis for selecting behaviour.

Like many controversies, this one between S–R and S–S theories proved to have no proper foundation. The theories were really about different aspects of the same problem and once the tangle of terminology was cleared up a conceptual resolution resulted. The rat possesses both a set of relationships between events that provide the basis for expectation, as well as a set of responses associated with stimuli which determine specific movements.

The artificial isolation of these theories was destroyed by the realisation that the experiments devised to test each of them tended to be specific to that theory. However, a reconstruction and combination of aspects of both theories was enormously encouraged when psychologists discovered cybernetics. This word derives from a Greek word meaning steersman and the field of knowledge that it distinguishes is the theoretical basis of control engineering.

The single most important concept in cybernetics is the feed-back loop. This informs a system about its own behaviour, and provides a basis for it to correct errors in its operation. Simple, familiar examples of such output-informed, self-correcting systems are the 'governor' on constant velocity engines and the thermostat which keeps the domestic oven at a chosen temperature. The key feature of systems like these is that the system works to produce a response that is sufficient to meet the demand of the signal which it receives. In principle, it does not have to 'know' what response to make since it can make random responses and eventually, when an adequate response occurs, that response can be maintained. The majority of engineering systems operating according to a negative feedback principle do so in one dimension and the system is programmed to respond appropriately according to the difference between feedback signal and demand signal. Thus if the steam engine is going too fast the governor reduces steam, if too slowly, it increases it.

The negative feedback loop offers a fruitful and plausible model for response-control processes ranging from choice to motor control. The evident involvement of visual feedback in threading a needle is more obvious than the corresponding involvement of 'predictions of effect on the environment' in the selection among alternative responses. However, both examples implicate the same basic feedback-loop error-correction processes. It is worth stressing again that the ideas of S–R and S–S theorists come together in this theory. The S–R contribution is to describe a basis for informed selection of responses in order to produce some effect, the S–S contribution defines the demand signals of successive and nested feedback systems and the predictions about the consequences of selecting particular responses.

Information-flow models

One of the effects of the impact of information theory and computer engineering on psychology has been to popularise attempts to conceptualise the processes underlying behaviour and the relations between them, in the form of an information flow diagram. The essential starting point is to consider the behaving organism as if it were a 'black box' that cannot be opened. It is then an exercise in scientific inference to deduce the functions which occur within it. Applications of this sort of approach to engineering problems are not unusual and one can expect to obtain mathematical solutions in the form of functional equations. Applications to psychological problems are less tractable. In effect, what happens is that the initial black box tends to be subdivided into a network of black boxes with lines between them to indicate the influences of one on another. For obvious reasons this exercise is sometimes known colloquially as 'boxology'.

In talking about models of psychological processes which are couched in these terms, it often helps to refer to engineering devices which act in a similar fashion, and are better understood. Such devices as the governor, thermostat and power-brake or power-steering systems make useful examples. However, there are glaring differences between the engineers' machine and comparable psychological processes. For example, the majority of negative feedback controlled servos operate continuously. There is a continuous relation between the operation of the steering-wheel and the movement of the road-wheels in a power-steering system. There may be a constant time lag (perhaps of only thousandths of a second) but control is continuous. The human being, however, in many instances appears to operate discontinuously. For example, in a task requiring continuous variation in response to match continuous changes in the input signal, subjects tend to change their response only about twice per second on the average. It is as if they process information in chunks, periodically. This is more like the way a digital computer operates. It takes time to carry out a computation and only after the central processor has been cleared can a new problem be tackled.

It is a consequence of this mode of operation that there have to be one or more stores of information to act as buffers. There is evidence to suggest that stores like this exist at both input and output. The system also requires access to information which has to be available on a long-term basis. A set of conditional relations is necessary to allow prediction of what will happen if a particular response is made. This is vital for the internal trial-and-error procedure used in selecting an appropriate response. It is also necessary for the system to store the program that governs its operation in a particular situation. The same system has to be able to drive a ten-ton lorry or a sports car, to play squash or table-tennis. If these similar but critically different activities are to be practised successively, there must be a change of programming of the system to ensure efficient operation. The software must be appropriately selected. Thus there are many ways in which information must be stored.

The study of memory has been mainly concerned with human verbal memory (see A6). However, it is clear that analyses of the kind rehearsed here indicate that non-verbal memory of different kinds is an essential attribute of the psychological system.

The use of information flow models as a method of unravelling the processes underlying behaviour is currently fashionable. It reflects the tendency of psychology to try any approach that might be fruitful. This particular one has a number of advantages which bode well. It has a mathematical basis which offers a quantitative technique when our thinking is sufficiently sophisticated to warrant it. The increasing availability of computers promotes the use of simulation as a procedure for testing the plausibility of models. Last but not least the possibility of discovering the physiological filling of at least some 'black' boxes means that hardware information could help the enterprise and encourages an integration of physiological with psychological theory.

8
Internal manipulations

The last chapter was devoted to a consideration of the processes involved in behaviour based upon a relatively direct relationship between input and output. In this chapter some attempt will be made to fill in the complex operations that can intervene. These are sometimes referred to as higher mental processes and include those processes which appear to be the special preserves of man. They are implied by complex behaviour and include the abstraction of concepts, the application of rules and deduction of consequences, and the discovery of solutions to problems. Many of these activities are called thinking (see A7). The layman uses thinking to refer to daydreaming as well. This activity, however, is usually not goal-oriented but rather a rehearsal of memories or the enactment of fantasies. The kind of thinking introduced here is that which is directed towards a well-defined end.

Symbols and symbolic manipulations

Even in the simpler through-flow varieties of behaviour considered before, the inner parts of the system were not conceived to respond to an external object directly; the response is to some internal representation. In so far as this representation stands in place of the object itself, it is a symbol. The processes involved in thinking require extensive manipulations of such symbols. They allow the system to make vicarious adjustments to the environment simply by manipulating its internal representations of the world. Their existence also divorces the representations of objects not only from the objects themselves but also from the normal constraints of space and time. Thus they provide the basis for both a sense of history and of predictions about the future.

The thesis offered here is that an organised symbolic system is the basis of language, and that language is, at least in part, a by-product of the evolution of a system for solving complex problems. It is seen as a natural though extreme progression from the processes discussed in chapter 7 which permit the selection of an appropriate pattern of muscle movements in order to produce a specific effect.

Language has two main components. First, there are the verbal symbols which are valuable only if there exists in memory a system of reference called semantics. Secondly, there are the rules of combination and ordering of the symbols, known as syntax or grammar. Those rules play a part similar to the rules which define how numbers can be manipulated in mathematics.

Until the last decade or so those psychologists who have studied language have been mainly concerned with its semantic aspects. They have sought to offer theories about both the role of words and also the ways in which they are learned. The dominant view has been to treat words as functionally similar to other internal representations or symbols which can become associated with particular referents according to the general rules of associative learning (cf. chapter 10). A psychological interest in syntax was stimulated by theoretical views about language developed by linguists. This initiative set the scene for the development of a new branch of psychology called psycholinguistics which aims to set linguistic ideas in a scientific context.

The view that words can be divided up into referential or content words and function words is attractive. Referential words are symbols for objects, attributes or relations which exist in the world. Function words such as 'but', 'some', 'through' and so on are added to the vocabulary because they play an essential part in the combination of referential words in sentences. They fulfil a function similar to addition and multiplication signs in algebra.

It is clear that, particularly for the acquisition of abstract words (those with no direct referent), the relation between a

95

sensory image and a word may be complex. Some abstract referents can only be tied to their symbols by a long process which leads to the evolution of that particular concept, and secondarily the application of a label. In contrast, learning to call a table 'table' involves a more direct identification of defining features which are then labelled.

After the first steps in learning referents have been achieved, the already learned referents can be used to acquire new ones. An adult tends to acquire new abstract referents from definitions couched in terms that he already understands. Eventually it seems that language learning can reach the point of independence of the physical referents upon which it was originally based.

This analysis highlights one important feature of internal representations either of objects or concepts. Language puts labels on them, but they need to exist before the labels can be applied. Even if labels are applied idiosyncratically and a word is improperly used, it nevertheless applies to something. The separate internal existence of a yet-to-be-labelled representation admits of the possibility that non-linguistic manipulations of these representations may occur. The contrast here is that between linguistic representations and imaginal representations. The latter may be the elements that form the basis for thinking in animals and pre-verbal children and may contribute to adult thinking. They are not thought of as images although they may provide a foundation for imagery.

This argument says no more than that thinking does not depend on language. However, it is clear that an organised system for handling internal representations confers a major advantage. It is in this way that language acts as a very potent aid to thinking.

Language acquisition

The approach adopted here is to stress the function of language as an aid to problem-solving. It also plays a more obvious role as a system of communication. It is, in fact, a very sophisticated system and though many other species have effective communication systems few, if any, have a well developed syntax that is the hall-mark of language. Animal communication systems seem to be limited to a referential system of symbols. Recent attempts to train chimpanzees to use symbols syntactically have met with only very limited success and, as yet, we must accept a more parsimonious explanation for the meagre skills they have learned.

The main puzzle about the acquisition of language concerns its syntax. It is clearly quite inconceivable that sentences are only learned by exposure to them. Children generate sentences they have never heard. Equally, a set of transitional probabilities (likelihoods of words given the preceding word) between words cannot account for the lawful language behaviour of young children. From a consideration of what children learn to do, as well as the systematic nature of the mistakes they make (e.g. 'two mouses'), it is clear that it is *rules* that are learned, rather than specific responses or response sequences.

Up to the mid-1950's psychologists tended to conceive of language as a form of sequential behaviour subject to the same rules as maze-running. This approach was rejected by linguists such as Chomsky, who stressed the dependence of language on the operation of generative rules. These ideas fell on fertile ground and many psychologists turned to the new field of psycho-linguistics. However, the early promise was not fulfilled. Chomsky's theories do not relate directly to linguistic performance, and it is hard to see if any data could exist that would disprove them. Nevertheless the scene has been set for the development of psychological theories that are free from the crippling defect of untestability.

The speed with which children normally acquire language, coupled with the similar basic form of a wide range of languages, has led some linguists to postulate the existence of linguistic universals (structural properties possessed by all languages). Furthermore, it is suggested that these universals are represented in the hardware of the brain; they are given to the child genetically. Armed with this basic information it is argued that the child has a predisposition to establish the kinds of rules which characterise language. These are challenging and contentious theories. They have proved a potent stimulus for research even if the matter is as yet unresolved.

Relations between language and perception

Whether one accepts the theory that some aspects of language are innate, or not, it seems evident that language must reflect experience, of the individual if not necessarily of his ancestors.

The relations which language is structured to reflect must be relations that exist and which are perceived. Language could in principle reflect relations that either do not exist or have not been perceived. ('How do you know that there are elephants in the fridge?' 'They leave their footprints in the butter.') But at the very least it must reflect those that have been perceived. In this sense language is determined by perception.

It has been suggested by Whorf that, in its turn, language can influence perception. This is known as the linguistic relativity hypothesis (see A7) which argues that thought is relative to the language in which it is conducted. The basis of this hypothesis is that different cultures have different powers of perceptual discrimination which are reflected by words in their language. For example, the Eskimo have words for different kinds of snow that a European can hardly tell apart. The Zuni Indians have colour names which refer to hues which differ from those with familiar English names. Both races do best on recognition tests of colours when remembering specific hues for which they have names.

Although the relation between perception and language is un-challenged, the implications are not straightforward. Snow is important to the Eskimo so it is necessary for him to learn to distinguish different kinds. The existence of different words helps to encode these varieties as well as to form communications about them. Though it is possible that the child may learn that there is more to snow than 'white stuff' because of the plethora of labels adults apply to it, the discrimination has to be perceptually based. It would seem unacceptably rash to con-clude that language determines perception. In any case, the existence of synonyms indicates that the existence of different words does not necessarily imply or impose a perceptual dis-crimination.

Problem-solving

This is a general heading which includes a number of different tasks. For example, the problem might be to discover the com-mon attribute which defines a class of objects. This is an ex-ample of *concept learning* (see A3). Subjects may be required just to respond appropriately or they may be required actually to articulate the rule in addition to acting in accordance with it. The former task may be achieved with the intervention of language as an aid but it is not necessary for language to be involved. Monkeys can acquire concepts.

Concept formation is one example of processing a quantity of information and deriving from it some overall generalisation. It is a vital step to take from specific exemplars to classes of objects, attributes or relations. It provides an essential stepping-stone to generalisation that enables solutions to particular problems to be applied to others of a like kind.

Deductive reasoning

A more obvious example of problem solving is reasoning. The prototype of this activity is the syllogism. Bound by the rules of formal logic, two related propositions lead unerringly to a conclusion. For example,

All fish are edible
All sea-creatures are fish
Therefore: All sea-creatures are edible.

The logic is sound but since both propositions are untrue the conclusion though logically perfect advises a foolish diet.

Deductive logic is a powerful tool. It offers well-defined rules of reasoning that expedite the testing of conclusions based upon initial propositions. It is a calculus for reasoning with rules which define the consequence of combining propositions. It is a kind of verbal mathematics. However, human reasoning tends to be subject to other considerations. Humans subscribe to a number of logical fallacies and thereby show that their reasoning system is not basically logical. Major instances of such illogical behaviour include atmosphere effects and acceptance of reverse propositions. For example the syllogism

All birds have wings
All robins have wings
Therefore all robins are birds

is logically incorrect even though each of the propositions is true and the conclusion is true. Acceptance of this syllogism is encouraged by the truth of its elements. The reverse proposition is of the kind

If p then q
therefore,
if q then p.

This confusion is more likely in some circumstances than others. For example, If it is daylight, then I can see. Such a proposition tends to lead to the reverse: If I can see, then it is daylight. However, If it is Sunday then the shop is closed, is much less likely to lead to the conclusion that, If the shop is closed then it is Sunday.

Logical reasoning is at the base of scientific thinking and essential for the development of the implications of theories and the evaluation of hypotheses. Humans left to their own devices tend to think in ways which transgress the rules of logic by being overly concerned with the plausibility of individual assertions. It is no surprise, therefore, that a scientific training entails the imposition of a special mode of thinking which is not a natural consequence of growing-up. Science depends upon the use of these logical rules, and they have to be learned.

Creative problem solving

It is possible that man's difficulties with thinking logically stem from his development of a different gift. This is to find solutions to problems which are open-ended. Either the tight logical system that characterises reasoning does not apply or, more probably, the context is inadequately defined to apply it. However, creative problem solving stands at the forefront of man's special skills and is at the base of his widespread technological prowess.

Problem solving is essentially concerned with drawing up ways of achieving specified ends. These range over the whole of human experience from persuading a recalcitrant child to eat, to determining a way of travelling between two towns. At the outset, it is fair to say that very little is known about how problems are actually solved. Four stages of the process have been described. These are preparation, consolidation, inspiration and evaluation. Unfortunately, the mysterious step between consolidation and inspiration remains obscure. Most of the work that goes on in solving a problem is hidden. It is not even approachable by introspection. Ideas which may prove to be solutions suddenly occur, though perhaps seldom with the dramatic impact that accompanied Archimedes' discovery of the principle of displacement. This phenomenon is probably not different in kind from the selection of a physical movement to bring about some desired effect – that too appears, but leaves no trace of its genesis.

Though successful problem solving occurs mysteriously, rather more is known about factors which inhibit it. It is also possible to propose a number of rules of thumb, which promote successful problem-solving behaviour.

If one is faced with a problem which does not immediately lead to a solution, it is likely that either additional information is required, or the information available needs to be reoriented. Psychologists have devised a number of laboratory tasks for investigating problem-solving behaviour. Some of these entail the manipulation of objects, others depend solely on internal, symbolic manipulation. Many of the former lead to solutions by putting the objects available to unusual uses. Difficulty in conceiving of other than the conventional use of an object is called 'functional fixedness' and is a major barrier to creative problem solving. Another important factor is 'set'. There is a strong tendency to apply a particular routine to a new problem if it has worked on similar problems in the past. In many instances, of course, 'set' is a valuable asset since it is a pointer to how the new problem might be solved. However, it proves to be difficult to put aside such a routine even when it evidently fails to work on the new problem.

Algorithms and heuristics
At least some aspects of problem solving are represented in games such as draughts or chess. In these cases there can be no information not available to the player, at least in theory. The difficulty of these games is due to the rich complexity of possible moves and counter-moves. In principle, a perfect game of chess could be played by systematically considering all possible moves. Such a strategy would be an algorithm, a system for enumerating every possible alternative. The application of an algorithm ensures solution of a soluble problem but, sometimes, at the cost of being prohibitively time-consuming. For example, even the most rapid computer could not play chess algorithmically, at least not against a human opponent, since the human being would not outlive the game!

Practical solutions to situations with such a rich set of alternatives need to use some corner-cutting methods. These are called heuristics. These are strategies, tricks or simplifications which, if appropriate will lead to the solution relatively quickly. The cost of this advantage is that they may not lead to any solution at all. Adopting an heuristic in place of an algorithm is often a gamble for that reason. In playing chess, however, there is no alternative. If a computer is to be programmed efficiently, and not just in an attempt to simulate human behaviour, it is necessary to establish within the program, heuristic sub-goals such as 'control the centre of the board', 'concentrate threats on the queen's bishop's pawn' and so on. One of the ways in which creative problem solving may be encouraged is to cultivate heuristics that may be of value in most situations. In mathematics it often helps to 'work backwards' from the algebraic 'solution', in practical problem-solving it is frequently useful to try to see the problem from novel angles when previously un-appreciated features may become evident.

Thinking is intrinsically a private process. No direct observation of it is possible. However, it is possible to devise experimental situations in which the consequences of this activity are manifested. Some progress has undoubtedly been made but further analysis of the complex covert processes involved in higher mental function will depend upon the ingenuity of researchers in devising experimental tasks which are capable of revealing them.

9
Go, goads, guidance and goals

It is time to complement the treatment of behaviour covered so far, with some discussion of the processes which are peculiar to organisms. These are answers to questions about how they come to do what they do. The primary questions concern the causes of variations in behavioural goals, why the organism does one thing rather than another, and how behaviour is guided along certain routes rather than others. The customary terms used to refer to the relevant underlying processes are motivation and emotion (see D2). Both words stem from the same Latin root, *movere*, meaning to move, disturb, change and to influence (the mind).

Homeostatic principles in behaviour. In the last three chapters it has been useful to consider behaviour as if it could be modelled on the operation of computers. However, computers and organisms differ in one important respect. A computer 'dies' when the mains plug is removed. The organismic equivalent of a mains plug is a very complex set of mechanisms and there is a built-in system for deferring its 'removal' for as long as possible. Some twenty years ago Grey Walter constructed a mechanical tortoise which ran on re-chargeable batteries. As the stored energy began to run low the tortoise put into operation a plan for getting its batteries recharged. This entailed finding a mains socket and plugging itself in; rather like a milk float which, with the help of a human operator, works in a similar way. The exciting aspect of Grey Walter's tortoise was its capability of activating a 'juice replenishing' system without human intervention. Of course, there is no magic about this. This feature of its 'behaviour' was built in during its design and construction. There are close parallels in human and animal behaviour, which also manifest such homeostatic principles (that is a tendency to make adjustments in order to return the system to some predetermined state).

Organisms deprived of basic life requirements will work to attain them. The essential needs for biological survival in mammals (the most intensively studied group of animals) include air, water and food. Deprivation of any of these will, sooner (if air) or later (if food) lead to a generalised increase in activity and a concentration of behaviour on the problem of acquiring them. If the organism has in its memory system an heuristic to guide it to a source of food or water etcetera, it will apply it. In short an organism will work for its own survival. Such behaviour implies that it has internal monitoring systems which detect critical deficiencies and a behavioural repertoire which is selectively energised on the occurrence of deficiency.

The dual function of motivation. It is a feature of living tissue to be spontaneously active. If the tissue has the complexity of an independently viable organism it will also have a repertoire of possible behaviours, only some of which can occur simultaneously. One of the functions of motivation is to select which of these behaviours occurs. The other primary function is a more general unselective raising or lowering of the tendency to act at all. This may be called 'arousal' and even though it has turned out to be a more complex concept than originally thought, it continues to be a useful way of referring to this general feature of the organism. Conditions which motivate have two effects; they have an arousal function and a selective function. In other words, motivation determines what an animal does and how vigorously it does it.

Emotion as an aspect of the motivational system. There is another side to this 'go and guidance' system. That is emotion. Emotion has two primary features. It refers to internal states which are 'feelings' and it also refers to particular behaviour patterns which reflect them. In a sense, emotion is an index of the state of the 'go and guidance' system.

Investigation of motivational and emotional processes has had natural recourse to a consideration of the physiology of the system. Such an approach is fairly obvious given the close links which are evident between physiological deprivation states (e.g. hunger) and behaviour. However, only the grosser aspects of motivation, and hardly any aspects of emotion, are made more comprehensible by the physiological knowledge that exists at present. Behaviour, and especially human behaviour, is subject to some very subtle influences, the majority of which have unknown physiological correlates.

Physiological needs and primary motives: the spirit is willing when the flesh is weak

The subtlety of behavioural influences makes it necessary conceptually to separate physiological need-states and the psychological drives which are the effective factors in determining the vigour and direction of behaviour. In general, biological needs are reflected in corresponding drives but there are also many drives which appear to exist without being linked in a direct way to a need-state. Drives which have a direct corresponding need are called primary drives. These include drives to sustain the existence of the organism in an intact form and also to maintain the species. Thus hunger-drive corresponds to the physiological need for food, thirst-drive to the need for water and pain avoidance (plausibly but not inevitably) to the need to avoid tissue injury. The sex-drive is also considered primary and has the function of encouraging behaviour which will ensure the continued existence of the species but the long lag between sexual behaviour and reproduction makes it very unlikely that the processes subserving sex-drive are as straightforward as those for hunger-drive. Since the timing of sexual behaviour is very much less critical than that of appetitive behaviour such as eating and drinking, it seems likely that it is controlled by somewhat different mechanisms.

Eating and drinking must occur relatively soon after the development of the relevant deprivation state. It is therefore appropriate for such behaviour to occur reactively. As such it is reasonable to search for a stimulus to such behaviour. This search suggests that blood glucose level and blood electrolyte balance and dilution, act as direct signals of needs for food and water respectively. Specialised areas deep in the brain have been shown to monitor these aspects of the blood. However, there is not a direct link between behaviour and changes in blood constitution. If there were, because of the time lag between eating and changes in blood glucose level, organisms would tend to gorge themselves on food instead of eating only enough for their needs. There is also the question of the mechanisms which lead animals to select different foods and, by so doing, achieve a balanced diet. Clearly, processes must intervene which have a predictive function and reduce the drive to eat when sufficient has been consumed eventually to restore blood glucose levels to desirable values.

The biological advantage conferred upon organisms that avoid and escape from injurious circumstances is obvious. It requires little imagination to appreciate that such well-equipped species would have a head-start in the natural selection stakes. The perception and anticipation of pain is perhaps at the closest coincidence between motivation and emotion. Pain produces massive effects on the motivation system imposing the greatest imperative on action, as it must if physical injury is to be minimised. In this sense it is the most urgent of the motivational states. It is also the supreme negative emotion with correspondingly massive incentive effects. The experience of extreme pain in particular circumstances may lead to traumatic avoidance learning with the result that the organism will never again approach those circumstances of its own accord. Some phobic responses in man may have this quality (see F3).

A number of motives though clearly conferring evolutionary advantage to their possessors do not seem to be associated with identifiable need-states. However, since they appear in the repertoire of all members of most advanced species (for example, mammals and birds) they are also listed as primary drives. These include the curiosity and investigatory motives which lead to a rat sometimes choosing the longer (and more interesting) of two routes through a maze it has learnt. Similarly, a chimpanzee will work to open the complex inter-locking latch system of a puzzle-box, extract the banana inside it, and then instead of eating the banana, replace it and do up the latches again! It is arguable that sex and maternal motives belong, at least in part, to this group as well. Both these kinds of behaviour are linked to hormone concentrations in the blood and in more primitive species they seem to be primarily determined by these physiological factors. However, in mammals, and especially in man, sexual and maternal behaviour is subject to more subtle influences. It is as if the choice of these kinds of behaviour is determined more by incentive than by a simple endocrinological stimulus.

Hedonic considerations

Explanations of the selection of investigatory behaviour would appear to be more satisfactory if couched in terms of a hedonic theory, a theory of satisfactions. Organisms indulge in these forms of behaviour because they are satisfying in themselves. The anticipation of such satisfaction then acts as an incentive. The hedonic quality of eating and drinking is also a potent incentive. Hedonistic theories were treated with suspicion by psychologists until the discovery of areas that could mediate hedonic states, situated deep in the brain (in the hypothalamus, quite close to the centres that monitor glucose and water concentrations in the blood). Electrical stimulation of these so-called 'pleasure' centres produces dramatic effects on behaviour. Animals, including man, will work exceptionally hard to be stimulated in this way and humans report that such stimulation produces feelings of intense pleasure. It is quite plausible that many different kinds of activity might culminate in internal stimulation of a pleasure centre which would confer positive value to those activities. Pleasure centres in the brain are complemented by pain centres which also have the quality of extreme intensity. Animals work to avoid stimulation in these regions, and humans report that artificial electrical stimulation there is intensely painful.

Emotion (or affective arousal as it is sometimes called) has been suggested as the basis of motivation. In essence, the organism acts to maximise positive affective arousal. This single axiom determines that it will seek out situations which promote that end and avoid those that jeopardize it. This conceptualisation conceives of emotion and motivation as indissolubly linked, emotion providing signals evaluating current and anticipated states of affairs. Behaviour is then considered to be organised about the basic axiom that pleasure is preferred.

Complex motives

A moment's thought is enough to appreciate that very little human behaviour can be accounted for in terms of the direct effects of primary drives such as hunger, thirst, pain termination, sex and the investigatory motives. This is probably also true of much mammalian behaviour. Therefore psychologists have sought ways of accounting for acquired drives. It is accepted that primary drives, certainly those directly connected to physiological need-states, could be genetically wired-in to the organism's hardware. If they were not, the species would not have survived the operation of natural selection.

The first major investigation of the development of an acquired motive was launched on the problem of avoidance behaviour. Rats will not only work to terminate a noxious stimulus such as an electric shock, they will also work to avoid it in circumstances where it may be anticipated. Some extension of the drive to terminate pain is necessary to account for this. Fear was proposed as the internal process, and postulated to motivate the avoidance response. It has the status of an acquired drive, is negatively evaluated and leads to avoidance behaviour. Fear is considered to be evoked associatively by the stimuli present during the application of the painful stimulus. That is, fear is an internal conditioned response (see p. 116). Fear is thus the anticipation of pain. Such conditioning has been offered as the basis for the acquisition of all secondary drives. Some further support is given by the discovery that chimpanzees can be trained to work a modified one-armed bandit for token rewards which can, later, be exchanged for bananas (a high-incentive positive reward).

The weakness of this formulation is that, at least in laboratory situations, the majority of learned motives seem to have a tendency to decline unless 'recharged' by further association with primary drive. One of the few experimentally induced secondary motives that may be an exception to this is traumatically induced fear. For example, dogs given one or two extremely strong electric shocks may continue to be fearful of the situation in which they were administered for as long as they are studied.

This is an important issue, for very little adult human behaviour is directly determined by physiological need and most of it is not determined by primary drives. Human behaviour is more dependent on such sophisticated concepts as needs for achievement, nurture, affiliation and so on. Some twenty-eight such psychogenic needs have been listed and the proposal that each arose out of direct association with primary drive is hardly credible. It is even less plausible that they should be maintained by continuing periodic association.

One possible escape from this impasse is a combination of an associative learning theory with the postulate that all motives (including acquired motives) may provide the basis for acquired motives. Further, having achieved some critical power a motive could become functionally autonomous, or self-sufficient, and thus need no further active maintenance.

Self-actualisation
Recent views about human motives have stressed man's awareness of himself as a person. Self-reference appears to be an important aspect. An individual will choose to act in a way which conforms to his desired self-image, which in its turn, will be a product of the cultural niche he occupies.

One of the attributes many people value is consistency. The avoidance of conflict between beliefs, for example, may be a potent motive for changing a discordant belief, or even distorting a percept. Festinger reports that the 'Seekers', having awaited the end of the world in vain, developed a new belief that the 'unstoppable' had been evaded by the power of prayer (see B1).

Maslow has attempted to construct a picture of human motivation that conceives of man as an aggregate of potentialities (see D1 and D2). There is axiomatically a pressure to develop them. He has proposed an hierarchy of five levels of needs to develop these potentialities. The basic needs are the physiological ones including food, water, sex and sleep. At the next level are the safety needs centred around the requirement of a predictable and orderly world. Next are the belongingness needs which govern friendships and interpersonal relations. Above these are placed the esteem needs including needs for achievement, independence and prestige. Topmost is the need for self-actualisation which is met only by full exploitation of talents and potentialities. Higher level needs are thought to be operative as determiners of behaviour only when lower level needs are reasonably well satisfied.

The nature of emotions

Emotion has been presented here as an essential aspect of motivation. It serves to guide behaviour, by virtue of its evaluative properties. However, it also has a communication function when expressed in a form that can be interpreted by other individuals. In this way, emotion serves a similar role to language which, in the last chapter, was discussed principally as a system for aiding problem-solving behaviour but which serves also the important role of a mediator in communication between individuals.

From our own experience we appreciate a broad spectrum of emotions. Attempts have been made to sketch out an emotional 'space' defined by named axes. One particular attempt proposes the dimensions of pleasant–unpleasant, level of activation (intensity) and interpersonal relatedness. Any one emotion is conceived as having a particular value on each of these dimensions and thus occupies a unique point in 'emotional space'.

Some attempts have been made to study the physiological correlates of emotional states. The strong emotions such as anger and fear have quite obvious physiological components. Sophisticated measurement of physiological indices such as heart rate, sweating and breathing rate indicate that systematic differences between fear and anger can be detected, even when these emotions are stimulated in a laboratory setting. Not surprisingly, most of this kind of research has been devoted to the strong negative emotions, because they are easier to induce. Whether all emotions are characterised by changes in such peripheral physiological indices is an open question. The possibility exists that in their normal operation, emotions are predominantly central states and that only in extremes of emotional arousal is there a spillage into the periphery.

Conflict

Conflict arises where two motives direct behaviour in mutually exclusive directions. Assuming that motives tend to promote either approach or avoidance behaviour, the principle conflict situations which can arise are as follows.

Approach–approach. This situation describes at least two alternative goals. The problem is similar to that of trying to catch two balls at once. The conflict is maximal if both goals have the same incentive value.

Avoidance–avoidance. This is the 'frying-pan and fire' situation. The problem becomes trivial if one can leave the field, so avoiding both consequences.

Approach–avoidance. In this case a single goal is considered to have both positive and negative qualities. Retreat means loss of the positive, approach means accepting the negative. The individual is trapped in the situation unless the incentive values are unbalanced, allowing a resolution of the conflict by a final response one way or the other.

Double approach–avoidance. This is the ultimate catch. Two or more goals exist, each with positive and negative attributes. Approach to any one leads to loss of the others in addition to the negative consequences associated with reaching the 'chosen' goal. Most of life's more difficult decisions are probably of this kind.

Frustration and aggression

Conflicting motives may inhibit a response, but in some instances goal-directed behaviour is prevented by some other kind of external barrier. For example, one may reach the bank at 3.29 p.m. on a Friday afternoon and have the doors close in one's face. In this case drawing cash for the weekend is thwarted by an over-punctual bank clerk. The result is both technically and experientially, frustration.

Thwarting barriers may be of many kinds. They may be physical like a locked door, procedural like 'use the correct forms completed in quintuplicate', geographical like the distance separating lovers, or social like 'not on the dining-table, please sir'. They may even be self-generated by a vigilant conscience.

Frustration has some of the attributes of motivation. For example it results in increased vigour in responding, at least in rats. It has also been identified as one of the principle precursors of aggression. The frustrated caller at the bank may knock on the door rather harder than necessary or, more likely, just swear. Reactive aggression of this kind may take different forms. It may result in an assault on the thwarting barrier. This is most likely if the barrier is a physical one. It may, otherwise, be displaced onto other objects (especially if the barrier is human or abstract) or it may even be internalised and turned against the self. There are clinicians who believe that some illnesses have psychological causes traceable to such intropunitive

111

reactions. Both the expression of aggression and its character-istic form is influenced by social factors. Until recently it might be said that the upper classes indulged in ritualised aggression, the lower classes gave vent to their feelings, while the middle classes gritted their teeth.

Arousal and performance

One of the dimensions of motivation is intensity. It is related to the vigour of behaviour and otherwise has been called level of activation or arousal. This has proved a fruitful psychological concept and particularly so with the prospect of discovering physiological measures that independently indicate arousal level.

Physiologists, however, are not agreed that a single dimension of arousal can be identified. The problem is that though several different indices of arousal have been found, such as heart rate, skin resistance, deep-body temperature, blood-pressure and so on, these several indices do not co-vary. The indices show arousal but not necessarily to the same stimulus conditions or at the same time. Nevertheless, the idea persists that a dimension of psychological arousal exists as a basic underlying state, even if the physiological indices do not reflect its action in a simple way.

One of the most striking beliefs about arousal and perform-ance is that the relation between them is not monotonic. That is, instead of there being a simple relation, such as performance increasing systematically with arousal, it is proposed that for any particular task there is an optimal level of arousal and if arousal rises above this point performance falls again. This is known as the inverted U-shaped relation, from its shape when graphed.

As a first approximation, this theoretical relation provides a valuable integrating function. It makes it easier to understand how both lack of sleep and loud noise can impair performance, yet noise will tend to improve the performance of a subject who is suffering from lack of sleep. There is even some evidence that some people (extraverts) tend to be normally aroused to a level below the optimum while others (introverts) tend to be chronically over-aroused. In consequence, loud noise may actu-ally improve the performance of extraverts while causing that of introverts to deteriorate.

This relation between arousal and performance is also relevant to the question of whether emotion is essentially constructive or destructive. The view taken here is that emotion is a natural concomitant of motivated behaviour. However, it may reach very high levels and, when it does, level of arousal will, by definition, also be very high. The inverted U-shaped function relating arousal to performance would lead to the expectation that while moderate levels of emotion may be an asset, very high levels will result in some breakdown of the performance of the system. In some circumstances 'cool it' would appear to be very sound advice.

10
Changing behaviour

Grey Walter's tortoise was remarkable for its capacity to pursue goals in an apparently purposive manner. However, it was also less flexible than almost any species of animal, since its behaviour did not change as a result of experience. This chapter is concerned with the principal ways in which changes of behaviour come about (see A3).

Habituation
Biological material tends to decline in its response to a constant stimulus. For example, pressure receptors in the gut and the joints tend to respond less and less as pressure upon them is maintained. This change is called *adaptation*. A change of stimulus and a short rest are sufficient for complete recovery of their sensitivity.

A superficially similar phenomenon occurs on a larger scale and involves the nervous system. Initially, contact lenses are exceedingly uncomfortable and can be tolerated for only a short time. However, if they are worn for increasing periods every day the eye-brain pain system eventually alters sufficiently for them to be used for most of the waking hours. Habituation has taken place.

Similarly a snail will retire into its shell if the surface on which it sits is vibrated. However, if this stimulus is repeated, the speed and degree of its retraction is progressively reduced until eventually it nonchalantly 'disregards' the stimulus altogether. If stimulation is omitted for a period, however, or the frequency of vibration is changed, the response will be evoked once more. Stimuli which cause the reappearance of habitual responses are said to produce dishabituation.

Somewhat higher up the evolutionary scale it may be shown that the orientation response to stimuli (pricking up the ears or turning towards the source of stimulation) tends to disappear with repeated presentation of the stimulus. However, habituation of this kind tends to be stimulus specific, as it is in the snail. A resting cat will respond on the first two or three occasions that one snaps one's fingers, but then, given no additional consequences, it comes to disregard the noise.

The value of habituation to the organism is evident if one assumes a principle of least effort. If a response is made which is in some sense anticipatory, either of injury (the pain from first wearing contact lenses), or of the imminent arrival of information (the mammalian orienting response), and the anticipated consequences fail to occur, the response is, in a sense, wasted. It would be efficient if the system selectively ignored such a stimulus. However, the anticipated implications of the stimulus might indeed transpire, so it would be efficient for the unresponsiveness to be maintained for only a limited period. Otherwise the snail might get eaten. Although it is possible to postulate an evolutionary justification for the habituation process, the mechanisms which underlie it are obscure. The occurrence of similar processes throughout practically the whole of the evolutionary scale suggests that habituation is one of the most primitive varieties of behavioural change.

Conditioning and learning

By far the greater part of research on learning has been conducted using non-human subjects. The choice of subject in these experiments has been determined by two principal considerations. First, there is considerable advantage in choosing a species that exhibits the behaviour to be analysed in as simple a form as possible. This may make it easier to study. The second factor has been to use a species that permits the use of rigorous controls. For example, many studies of learning behaviour require careful control of the motivating conditions and the past experience of the subject. It is also important to use subjects who are amenable to the experimental procedures. For these reasons, and because they are relatively cheap to procure and maintain, psychologists have performed many of their experiments on white or 'hooded' rats. (Their next most favourite subject has been the U.S. college sophomore, though not for quite the same reasons!) It has to be recognised at the outset that there is some danger in uncritically generalising from the results of experiments on rats to predictions about the processes underlying human behaviour. However, there is ample evidence that although humans may possess processes (such as language) that distinguish them from rats, at least some aspects of human behaviour reflect the operation of processes indistinguishable from those governing rat behaviour.

As in the investigation of other hypothetical mental processes, there is no opportunity to view the processes underlying learning and memory in isolation. In the case of learning, the behaviour that is observed is also dependent upon the operation of perceptual and memory processes. In fact the difference between studies of learning and of memory is really only one of emphasis. The distinction is between manipulating the conditions effective around the time of registration and those effective when the subject is called upon to perform. In the main, most 'learning experiments' have used animal subjects, whereas most 'memory experiments' have been conducted on human subjects.

Varieties of learning

Two main classes of learning have been identified (see A3). They are distinguished by the procedures involved in their laboratory study and, to some extent, by being characterised by different phenomena. The first of these classes is variously known as classical conditioning, Pavlovian conditioning and respondent conditioning. It is distinguished procedurally by the presentation of two stimuli to the subject. One, the unconditional stimulus, has the effect of eliciting a particular response called the unconditional response. For example, food in the mouth induces salivation; a bright light produces contraction of the pupil of the eye. During classical conditioning training, this unconditional stimulus is normally preceded by another stimulus, the conditional stimulus, that prior to training does not produce the unconditional response. Repeated trials on which the conditional and unconditional response are presented, eventually lead to the elicitation of a response by the conditional stimulus.

The form of this conditional response is similar to the unconditional response. For instance, if a bell precedes placing food in the mouth, eventually the subject will salivate to the bell alone.

The other kind of learning is called operant conditioning or instrumental learning and has been most closely associated with B. F. Skinner. A typical training trial comprises the presentation of a 'reward' to the subject if he makes the desired response. Little attempt is made to elicit the desired behaviour, but instead 'spontaneously' emitted behaviour is selectively reinforced by the experimenter. The classical apparatus for studying learning of this kind is the Skinner box which is characterised by some kind of manipulated component such as a lever, which the subject can press, and some kind of device for delivering the 'reinforcer'. Depending upon the procedure adopted (the degree of selectivity of reinforcement) the response of the subject can be made to occur specifically in conjunction with particular stimuli. For example, a pigeon may be trained to peck a key when it is red but not when it is green. A much less discriminatory situation might lead a rat to press the lever whenever it is available. The relations between stimuli and response which result from this training regimen are determined by the reinforcement contingencies imposed by the experimenter.

There are obvious differences between these kinds of training. In classical conditioning, the unconditional stimulus is presented on every training trial so that the unconditional response is elicited on every trial. Presentation of the unconditional stimulus is not contingent on the subject responding to the conditional stimulus in a particular way. In contrast, the reinforcer in instrumental conditioning is only presented on the occurrence of the response that has been selected for training. These two types of learning have elements in common. For example, systematic omission of the unconditional stimulus after training will cause the conditional response to decline in vigour and, eventually, to disappear. This procedure is called 'experimental extinction'. Similarly, omission of reinforcement in the instrumental learning paradigm also leads to a reduction in the probability of emission of the operant response. Clearly, in these situations, behaviour is controlled by the unconditional stimulus and the reinforcer respectively.

Further parallels may be discerned between these two acquisition processes. In classical conditioning the unconditional stimulus elicits the unconditional response, and the goal of training is achieved when the unconditional response comes to be elicited by the conditional stimulus. Operant training omits a stimulus which reliably elicits the response which is desired. Instead, the experimenter has to wait until the response is spontaneously emitted before applying reinforcement to it. This wait could be an extremely long one and, in order to expedite learning, a 'shaping procedure' is adopted. This entails reinforcing a response which is emitted reasonably often at the beginning of training, and then selectively reinforcing behaviour which approaches increasingly closely to the target response. Patient and ingenious use of shaping procedures can lead to the development of very unusual behaviour patterns, such as chickens playing a version of table-tennis!

The key concept in instrumental learning is that of reinforcement. The reinforcer is clearly the potent variable which determines behaviour. Behaviour may be manipulated by altering the reinforcement contingencies. The range of behaviour which is vulnerable in this way is very wide indeed, if not comprehensive. For example, reinforcement contingencies can affect not only pigeons pressing keys but also the preference of human beings for particular grammatical construction in speech (such as active versus passive or plural instead of singular nouns). The effects of different contingencies of reinforcement (known as schedules of reinforcement) have been intensively studied. Continuous reinforcement (the reinforcer is presented on every trial) seems intuitively to be the most potent form. However it turns out to lead to behaviour which is less stable than partial reinforcement (in which the reinforcer is presented on only some of the occasions when the desired response is emitted). An excellent example of partial reinforcement is that provided by the one-armed bandit or fruit machine.

These two kinds of learning have been advanced as examples of two basic processes underlying changes in behaviour. They have also been allied selectively to different classes of behaviour. Classical conditioning has been postulated as the basis for changes in responses controlled by the autonomic nervous system. These responses are normally involuntary and include changes in the activity of glands, gut motility, blood vessels and so on. In contrast, responses controlled by skeletal muscle contractions and under the influence of a different sub-division of the peripheral nervous system, are considered to be subject to operant training procedures. In consequence it is often said that involuntary behaviour (including much emotional behaviour) is classically conditioned, whereas voluntary behaviour is learned instrumentally. This distinction is probably over-simple but provides a reasonable working rule.

Learning, performance and reinforcement

One of the main questions about learning that has been asked repeatedly during the last fifty years has concerned the function of reinforcement. Operationally it changes the probability of the learned response, but how it does so is less obvious. One major theory asserts that reinforcement acts through the reduction of a drive. This view provides a definition which allows reinforcers to be predicted; they are those stimuli which reduce drives. For example, food reduces hunger-drive and is therefore a potent reinforcer. However, the association between drive reduction and reinforcement is more difficult to discern at human level where most natural reinforcers are social, such as a word of praise, a smile, or even rapt attention. It seems more likely that reinforcers are no more than desired states of affairs, which is an hedonic view of reinforcement. It is relevant to consider that electrical stimulation of a 'pleasure centre' deep in the brain is probably the most potent reinforcer yet discovered.

This problem is complicated by the logical distinction between learning and performance. It may be that a reinforcer acts on performance rather than on the learning process directly. This problem is particularly sharpened if learning is conceived as the formation of associations between stimuli (including internal stimuli) and responses (including internal responses). S–R chains including complex feed-back loops can be developed to great complexity and may provide a satisfactory analysis of even very complex behaviour. The distinction this points up is that between the formation of an association and its activation. Different factors may act on these two processes.

In general, performance depends upon incentives which are provided by the expectation of reinforcement. The *formation* of links between internal states and responses, however, may be purely associative, based upon temporal contiguity. This view conceives of learning as simply lubricating a particular network

119

so that it may be traversed more easily next time round.

It has been questioned whether classical conditioning and instrumental learning exhaust the forms of learning that are manifest in human behaviour. Specifying the reinforcers for learning to play tennis, a telephone number, or the contents of this book seems rather more difficult than in the case of lever-pressing in a Skinner box. Humans internalise the world to a greater extent than other animals and the possibilities of self-reinforcement conferred by language are potent. It seems that achievement of a new skill may be sufficient an incentive to learn it. The analysis of human behaviour in terms of basic concepts such as reinforcement, motive and incentive is a major challenge. But it is too early to conclude that such an analysis must fail without the introduction of additional processes.

Human learning

At the human level the two principal forms of learning that have been studied are verbal learning and the acquisition of motor skills. Although sweets are sometimes used as reinforcers in experiments on children, the most common reinforcers are social ones such as praise, or personal esteem ones such as reports of good performance. The motives that are operating to control human behaviour are clearly somewhat more complex than in the rat. However, it has been assumed that there is functional equivalence between a food-pellet to a rat and knowing he has made the correct response, to a human.

Guidance

The two principal ways of manipulating learning behaviour in humans are feedback and guidance. Guidance is functionally similar to shaping in the instrumental learning paradigm. By restricting the variety of responses that are either physically possible or likely to be made, the subject is constrained to produce a response which is reasonably close to the one which is desired. The constraint may be physical or psychological. For example, a good golf-swing may be encouraged by using a system of wires which limits the movement of the golf-club to an arc which is the theoretical ideal. The pupil, by using this apparatus, can learn what a good swing feels like and practise the sequence of muscle contractions which produces it.

Psychological constraint may take many forms varying from verbal instruction to carry out a series of actions that are already under voluntary control, to the presentation of a behaviour model that may be copied. It is unlikely, however, that the way in which guidance ensures that behaviour early in the learning comes within sight of the final objective, has much to do with what is ultimately learned by the subject. Guidance frequently entails artificial aids to performance that are not normally available. The subject has to learn to perform without them and to depend only upon cues which are intrinsic to the task itself. However, different kinds of guidance provide various opportunities for the subject to learn what aspects of the environment and of his internal (proprioceptive) world he should attend to. It may also encourage the selection of an appropriate set of acts that already exist in his repertoire, and define the sequence in which they should be assembled.

Feedback
Feedback is the process by which a system is informed of its output. In human learning this simply means informing the subject of the outcome of his actions. Feedback may be of several kinds. It may be intrinsic to the task or it may be artificially added to it. Augmented feedback is often used early in learning a complex skill before the more subtle intrinsic feedback signals have become discriminated. Feedback may take the form of knowledge-of-results in which case it is likely to be somewhat delayed in time and may be only weakly related to the actual responses made by the subject. For example, at the end of several trials an overall appreciation of accuracy may be given instead of trial-by-trial feedback. Feedback may also vary in its precision. It is more informative to a subject to know that his arrow missed gold by landing twenty-five centimetres to the right and eighteen centimetres too low, than just being told he scored an inner. In some ways, feedback or knowledge-of-results appears to fulfil the function of reinforcement in an instrumental learning paradigm.

Verbal learning
The problem of understanding human learning is evidently a complex one. It is not surprising that most research effort has

121

been concentrated on relatively simple tasks, on the assumption that once they have been understood it will be easier to tackle more complex ones. The all-pervading influence of language on human behaviour makes it natural that verbal learning, even in a simple form, should be the preferred kind of learning to study. Two main kinds of task have been studied. One concentrates on the formation of associations between words and is called paired-associate learning. The other is concerned with the learning of sequences of words. In fact, both tasks have general relevance since paired-associate learning could be considered the basis of associative learning in general, and serial learning is an example of the way in which orderly sequences of responses of any kind may be learned.

It has become clear that learning proceeds by stages. Initially it is necessary for the subject to learn what responses are relevant in a particular task. This is called response learning. This may entail learning how to make the responses themselves (that is, acquiring a particular skill) or it may simply involve determining which of all the responses in his repertoire are relevant. The second stage requires that the subject learn when to make these responses. Typically this means defining the context in which they should be made. This latter is called associative learning. Clearly the difficulty of learning a particular task will be divided between these two subsidiary problems. A question that has engaged a number of researchers concerns the nature of these forms of learning.

Studies of learning inevitably rely upon the operation of memory since without it no evidence of learning could exist. Verbal learning experiments typically involve multi-trial procedures in which the same material to be learned is presented repeatedly. One measure of learning is to score how the subjects' performance improves trial-by-trial. This gives rise to a learning curve. By conducting experiments in which the material or the structure of the task are varied, or in which the conditions prevailing before, during and immediately after presentation of the material are manipulated, the research is concentrated on the learning process. However, by concentrating on the conditions prevailing when learning is tested (by recall or recognition, for example) or by manipulating the events which intervene between presentation and testing, experiments can be conducted which emphasise memory.

Memory processes

Experimental enquiries about memory have concentrated on attempts to discover the nature of the processes which underlie the ability to retrieve information. Some work has been done on the underlying physiological systems. Most of this work has been conducted on animals and directed at the form of information storage. By using traumatic procedures such as electro-convulsive shocks applied to the brain or the application of chemicals to the surface of the brain, as well as the selective surgical removal of areas of the brain, some aspects of the physiology of memory have been revealed. For instance, jazzing-up brain function with massive electrical stimulation appears to prevent the effects of recent experience leaving a lasting 'trace'. Somewhat earlier experience, however, is little affected by such treatment. It would seem that a period of consolidation may be necessary to allow permanent memory traces to become established. These observations may be stored in two ways: a dynamic functional trace that is vulnerable to stimulation from electrical and chemical stimuli, and more durable structural traces that remain even after brain activity has been totally suppressed by a reversible cooling procedure.

This two-process theory of memory finds parallels in human memory research which has for some time stressed differences between the processes underlying short-term as opposed to long-term memory. The parallels should probably not be drawn too closely. The time relations may be quite different and the psychological distinctions between short-term memory and long-term memory are not logically related to the physiological evidence.

Studies of human memory indicate that a subject's ability to recall past events changes with the amount of time elapsing between presentation and recall. Immediate recall tends to include much greater detail and frequently 'feels' easier since there is very little reportable use of searches through the memory system. When recall is delayed for several minutes or longer, the information retrieved is much less like an exact copy of that which was presented. Instead, it is as if the original information has been digested and what is recalled is some organised version of it. One way of studying the codes used by the memory system, is to examine the kinds of errors that are made. It is assumed that incorrect responses are chosen because

123

they resemble, in important ways, the correct response. It follows that the dimensions of the coding system may be inferred from the nature of memory errors.

It is found that as the retention interval increases memory errors change in form. Immediately after presentation, memory errors are like perceptual errors. For example, acoustic confusions abound in the immediate recall of strings of letters. Letters that sound alike may be interchanged. However, errors based on semantic similarity (that is similarity of meaning) dominate at longer retention intervals. The inference from these sorts of observations is that different memory codes or 'languages' are involved. Some theorists have gone further and concluded that different processes exist which they represent by different 'boxes'. Others have argued for a unitary system, but one which is organised in a series of levels, each level having its own defining characteristics.

One of the important distinctions between the processes available to memory in the short-term and the long-term, is the durability of the information they carry. The post office exhorts subscribers to write down telephone numbers before dialling them. This advice is important because the act of dialling takes so long that there is a real risk of forgetting the number, or getting the constituent digits in the wrong order. Of course, everyone knows some numbers 'by heart'. There is no difference between the nature of the material that may be stored in transient and in permanent storage systems, only between the forms of its representation.

Although a considerable amount of memory research has been devoted to trying to understand the basic features of the system, psychologists are becoming increasingly aware of more complex problems. There are strategies used by some people to 'improve' their memories. Some of them entail very sophisticated schemes for integrating the new information with an informational structure that is already stored. These schemes are called mnemonics. Their effectiveness raises some interesting questions about the operation of memory. Like so many behavioural phenomena, we tend to notice rather more when the system fails. From a scientific point of view the way it goes wrong is often a fruitful source of ideas about how it works normally. As laymen we are more concerned when we cannot remember something than we are about the astonishing way in which we do remember things.

It would seem at the outset that failures in recall could be attributed to failing to register the information initially, to it being distorted or even destroyed after having been stored, or to inefficiency of the retrieval mechanism. All of these sources of 'forgetting' may affect everyday performance. However, the context in which information is registered probably determines both the resistance of the stored information to interference from subsequent events and the efficiency of retrieval. The use of a good mnemonic ensures that the new information is integrated within an existing network of information and, provided one remembers the mnemonic, a retrieval system for recovering the information later is also specified. For example, given the sentence 'Richard Of York Gained Battles In Vain', one may, from the initial letters, reconstruct the order of the spectral colours: red, orange, yellow, green, blue, indigo, violet.

It is quite possible that non-verbal systems for remembering things are more powerful than verbal mnemonics. The original Greek advice on how to learn things was to incorporate them into an image of some kind. Simonides described the use of a strategy that involved locating each object or event in a room in a mental image of a familiar house. Retrieval entailed searching mentally through the rooms of the house. Other imaginal methods of integrating information depend upon combinations of ideas into an image. For example, the somewhat unconnected words 'string, flute, basket' may be incorporated into a cartoon of the Indian rope trick. These examples are described in terms of visual images. It is not proposed that non-verbal imaginal representations are necessarily in this form. However, these examples point up the distinction between verbal and imaginal representations. Both are probably essential components of the human memory system.

Considering the difficulty we have in learning multiplication tables or telephone numbers, some feats of memory seem remarkable. For example, several experiments have demonstrated that even if presented for only a second or two, several hundred pictures of natural scenes (landscapes, portraits and so on) can be correctly recognised and distinguished from other similar pictures, with only perhaps ten per cent errors. This kind of performance is unlikely to be the result of mnemonics of the 'Richard of York' variety. Too little time is available for the development of such a scheme for each picture. Instead, it would seem that the memory system automatically encodes new visual information in such a way that, at least in terms of recognition, it is efficiently remembered.

Current memory research is turning increasingly away from the use of isolated items and events and moving closer to everyday situations, by studying memory for connected prose and for pictorial material. In this way memory research is converging on some of the questions raised in considering higher mental processes, in chapter 8. An important distinction between verbal and imaginal representations was alluded to there. These distinctions seem equally essential in considerations of memory.

11
Psychological psychology

Science proceeds on two legs. One leg is empirical enquiry, the other is the development of theories. Theory is adjusted in the light of empirical data. This description of the march of knowledge implies an intrinsic goal which is, in some sense, the perfect truth. A more realistic appreciation would shrink this goal to the more practical one of 'a truth'. There is some hope of achieving this more limited level of understanding. In fact, it may be attained repeatedly, since truths may be conceived of at sundry different levels, and each be as true as the others. This chapter is concerned with the progress made by psychology towards this particular 'holy grail', including some of the pitfalls that may await the unwary explorer.

Theories and facts

The real world may or may not be designed according to a master-plan from above. It is, however, orderly in the sense of being non-random in form. Given lawfulness then the discovery of the laws is a challenge that may quite reasonably be expected to be successful. In psychology, the most obvious laws are those relating behaviour to prior and contemporaneous conditions. One level of truth would be achieved if those laws were to be adduced. Another level of truth concerns the nature and mode of function of the processes which cause that functional relation. Science progresses by offering best guesses about the answers to these questions. These guesses are called theories or models. It is not anticipated that theories will be 'the truth', but only an approximation to it at a particular level.

A consequence of this *modus operandi* is that theories are always analogues of the real world. As such, several different theories may be equally acceptable even though couched in very different terms, provided only that the closeness of the analogy is the same. The goal, of course, is to develop a model which is valid at a deeper level of understanding than any yet achieved. One means of doing this may be to change the 'language' or form of expression of the model. Such a step may overcome current limitations associated with a particular 'language'. An example of this in psychology is the adoption of some of the concepts of cybernetics and their application to learning situations, which had previously been dominated by S–R learning theories. The feedback concept was not discovered recently, nor was its application in psychology the stimulus for this change (Troland even gave the concept another name, 'retroflex', as early as 1928). Cybernetics, however, offers a different level of conceptual development and a mathematical base that has great potential.

The function of theory is to impose order on data and to provide an organisation from which predictions can stem. Theories may vary in the depth to which they plumb, they also vary in terms of breadth. This distinction is sometimes drawn between maxi-theories and mini-theories. The former make assertions about variables and processes that have general application and influence a wide range of behaviour. The latter are more circumscribed in their ambit. For example, theories of personality such as Freud's (D3), and classical learning theories such as Hull's (A3), are maxi-theories. Mini-theories include Atkinson and Shiffrin's model of memory (A6) and Broadbent's model of selective attention (A4).

On the generality of explanatory concepts

Examination of psychological ideas suggests that they change as there is a move away from observed behaviour and towards more fundamental covert underlying processes. Essentially, psychological concepts are only peculiar to psychology when they relate to superficial aspects of behaviour. Raw descriptions of and first order generalisations from data fall into this category. However, as soon as concepts are employed at an explanatory level, in the development of ideas about the processes which produce the behaviour, then clear similarities are obvious between them and concepts used in other disciplines.

The switching of attention which determines the input to a one-job-at-a-time central processing mechanism in Broadbent's filter model of attention is immediately familiar. It calls up the behaviour of electrical circuits, general physical 'truths' about pints going into half-pint pots, and the fact that everything takes time. The use of feedback concepts has already been described. However, they are more rigorously used in engineering and can hardly be claimed as psychological.

This generality of concepts is not restricted to those psychological enquiries which are the province of this book and this section in the series. Freud's theories about unconscious processes entail concepts of force and reaction that are basically those employed in physics. Theories of attitude change based on the idea of an equilibrium use the same concept that is otherwise applied in physics and chemistry. Even the long-standing concept of the associative bond, which by now has enjoyed a life of about two thousand years, is not essentially different from the bonds that chemists suppose to join atoms together, or, on occasion, the statistical sequence that is the hall-mark of causation.

Rules of correspondence

The force of these observations is that at most level of theorising the essential concepts are not specific to a particular subject matter. As a consequence, theories have two main features. The theory itself asserts a set of relations between named entities. This describes how these entities or variables interact and provides the ground for prediction. In addition to this, however, if the theory is ever to be tested or applied, an additional set of rules is required to relate the corpus of the theory to the real world. For example, if a theory makes statements about the relation between stimulus and response, no progress can actually be made unless both stimulus and response are unambiguously, operationally defined. These rules are called rules of correspondence. Sometimes they are, or at least they seem to be, self-evident. Perhaps one of the troubles that psychology has suffered is that its theories have not always bothered enough about rules of correspondence, with the result that personal interpretations differ from researcher to researcher. One of the main weaknesses of the Hullian S–R theory of learning and performance was the lack of explicit rules of correspondence, which left an elegant theory concerning processes only vaguely anchored to observable input and output. Just what was a stimulus or a response had to be determined by the user of the theory.

The autonomous existence of theories

It is this weakness that gives theories their longevity. The myth of science is that theories are developed to account for data. Data are collected to test such theories further and should data conflict with theoretical expectations, the theory is either changed to accommodate the new information or it is jettisoned. The latter action creates a vacuum into which some new theory may move. In fact, theories very seldom receive an empirical *coup de grâce*. It has been said that theories, like old soldiers, only fade away. A competing theory is a far more potent force in this respect than incompatible data.

Such invulnerability to disproof stems from two sources. First is the point already made. Sloppy rules of correspondence make critical tests of a theory difficult if not impossible to mount. It is always open to the proponent of the theory to argue that the embarrassing data lie outside the domain covered by the theory, or alternatively that the predictions from the theory were improperly related to data. With the wisdom of hindsight it is then possible to show how there is, in fact, no conflict between theory and data. The second source of difficulty in testing theories is a statistical one. In psychology the majority of 'facts' are inferred from 'noisy' data that have to be submitted to sophisticated statistical analyses to reveal systematic features. Statistics makes assumptions of its own about the nature of the data (see A8) and the 'facts' that emerge from the analysis may be influenced by the validity of those assumptions. Furthermore, the majority of conclusions from the application of statistical analyses are probabilistic. In other words, there is a small but finite probability (say one in twenty or one in a hundred) that a particular result could have been due to chance variation rather than a real effect. Thus data may not always provide the unassailable, ultimate, factual criterion that they are often supposed to be.

In many instances recourse is had to data in order to settle a dispute between rival theories. A conflict model of scientific advance has considerable application. Because of the difficulties outlined above, a competing theory proves to be a far more potent stimulus to empirical enquiry than are embarassing data. It is, of course, recognised that no theory about the world can be proved. Proof is only possible in a deductive sense and thus only applicable to a closed logical system. Disproof, however, is another thing. A single black swan is sufficient to disprove the assertion that 'all swans are white'. The strategy behind an empirical choice between theories is based on the concept of finding data which relate to both theories and which are incompatible with one of them. Once again the importance of rules of correspondence is emphasised. It is vital that the two or more theories under consideration should all relate to the observation in question.

Confirming instances. Scientists, being human, and faced with such difficulties in establishing the implications of negative data, are also concerned with confirming as well as disconfirming evidence. There is an obvious preference between two theories, one of which has yet to be disconfirmed while the other is supported by confirming evidence. The value of confirming observations becomes more obvious when one considers that many psychological hypotheses are probabilistic in nature. It is more often than not a question of 'most swans' rather than 'all swans' being white. In this case it is the relative number of swans of different hues that is critical, and a few black swans have little effect on the credibility of the assertion.

Unfortunately this justification for considering positive as well as negative instances can lead to a false evaluation of theories. Consider a theory which predicts an event A, as opposed to other events B, C and D. An observation is made and A occurs. How does this affect the theory? Does it make it more likely to be true? The answer is that it may do. Whether it does or not depends upon what alternative theories predict. The relation between a particular theory and a confirming instance is only part of the story. This complication arises because all possible theories might predict the observation of event A. In such a case, the occurrence of A has no effect on the relative credibility of any one theory. Of course the non-occurrence of A is just as informative as ever. It would indicate that all the theories under consideration were wrong.

The need to consider the predictions made by possible alternative theories obviously makes more complex the problem of testing a particular theory. It has made some evaluations of psychological theories very difficult. Eysenck (1972) has explored this problem in relation to attempts to test aspects of psychoanalytic theories of personality. Many so-called empirical confirmations of these theories are unconvincing because one or more competing theories would make identical predictions. The occurrence of results that an experimenter hoped to obtain does not necessarily herald confirmation of his theory.

In short, it appears that theories can take on an existence which is almost independent of data. For data which appear to negate the theory may be quite easily rejected as irrelevant or a chance effect. At the other extreme, data that are turned to in confirmation of a theory have very little weight unless few, if any, other theories also make the same prediction.

Fads and fancies
Though it may be true that theories are seldom, if ever, jettisoned on the grounds of the existence of disconfirming data, theories are supplanted all the time. One of the factors which operates might be called intellectual fashion. It has been argued that theories never really gain general recognition out of their time. The climate has to be right. As a consequence it is common to find a number of independent researchers coming up with the same sorts of ideas at the same time, and charges of plagiarism are not necessarily deserved. Ways of thinking and conceptions of various global features of the discipline, change all the time. These changes are seldom dramatic revelations but, over perhaps a decade, the appearance of the subject may alter radically. Psychology is particularly subject to variations in interest of this kind and to changes in the sorts of theory which are accorded special respect.

Instances of this are legion. Introspection enjoyed its major vogue from the 1870's to about 1920 when the tide of behaviourism overwhelmed it. Behaviourism, as described by Watson, appeared to deny the validity of verbal reports and they did not regain respect until some thirty years later. The development of high-speed computing machines and high-level programming languages made machine analogies and information-processing models fashionable. These are now giving way to less mechanistically inclined views of the subject that stress his essentially active nature. These changes have taken place without being stimulated by the exhaustion of a rich vein of psychological ore. Fashions have overtaken research and the unfinished tends to become the neglected.

Changing conceptions of subjects

Sophisticated mechanical toys which can be constructed to mimic various aspects of behaviour have an intrinsic interest for psychologists. No doubt one reason for this is that when one's theoretical ideas are realised in hardware terms and then tested without being found wanting, the credibility of one's ideas is greatly enhanced. Although logically there is no difference between Grey Walter's tortoise and Weiner's analysis of cybernetic systems, the former is the more immediately and directly convincing. The more complex the behaviour produced in this way, the more convincing the demonstration. An adaptive program for computerised chess-playing invests its creator with great respect, even though it may play chess using processes which differ in many important ways from the human master.

Analyses of motivation stressed the essential activity of living tissue. Motives modulate and direct this basic attribute. The popularity of information-processing approaches to the analysis of behaviour has been so great that this essential fact has been pushed into the background. Even the conception of the nature of the human subject has been altered. Machines are not spontaneously active. They operate in a pre-ordained fashion on information which is input to them. Their behaviour, though complex and sometimes apparently unpredictable, is the result of a formulated program. It is tempting to conceive of the subject in a psychological experiment in the same way. He is 'programmed' by his genes, his experience and the particular instructions that relate to the experiment in which he partakes. It would be nice to think that he does as he is told to do. Most of the time he probably does not.

This picture of a passive information-processing subject is another myth. The truth is that subjects indulge their own motives by serving in experiments and act to maximise their satisfactions. If their need to cooperate is sufficiently strong they will indeed attempt to follow instructions but the instructions they follow will be their own idiosyncratic interpretation of those given by the experimenter. These two versions may not always correspond. Other subjects may enter the experiment in a spirit of competition instead of cooperation. Their goals may not be at all like those of the experimenter. Finally, and a slightly different point, the strategies (consciously reportable or otherwise) employed by subjects in an experimental situation may be neither common nor consistent. There are, after all, individual differences even in the processes used in such simple arithmetic operations as subtraction.

The challenge to the experimenter is to design and conduct his experiments in such a way that the resulting data are unequivocal in their implications. It is very difficult to meet this challenge successfully. Those who customarily work with non-human subjects enjoy two main advantages. First, there is for them no short-cut to preparing subjects for an experiment. They have to be painstakingly trained. (The dangerously attractive alternative with human subjects is to read a set of verbal instructions. It is quick but is it sufficiently effective?) The second advantage is that the experimenters are substantially brighter than their non-human subjects and are almost certain to be able to out-think them. The human experimenter working with human subjects has a barely better than even chance of coming out on top. Perhaps human experimentation could be made less equivocal by introducing some of the 'instructional' procedures typically used in animal research, thereby reducing the unwanted initiative shown by individual subjects given verbal instructions.

The concept of the 'active' subject who is capable of programming himself is one reason to look more closely at the rigour of experimental control. It is particularly apposite to consider this when psychology is showing increasing interest in the more complex mental processes which distinguish man. It is obvious that there is more room for individual initiative in sentence comprehension or semantic memory than in detecting a faint unstructured stimulus. In consequence it is more difficult to design good experiments (that is, unequivocal as opposed to interesting experiments) in these increasingly popular areas of research.

Experimenter expectancy effects

As if these cautions were not enough, it would be a major omission not to discuss sources of direct artefact in experimentation. The problems of interpretation that arise when one experimental variable is confounded with another are the main stimuli for applied statisticians to develop experimental designs and the sophisticated statistical analyses necessary to make sense of the data that they produce. However, more recently, the experimenter himself has been identified as one potent source of artefact, and the reactions of subjects to their perceptions of what the experimenter expects or wants to find, another.

Some experimenter effects are very subtle but systematic distortions of the data. Even reading a measuring instrument may be subject to such an influence. If rounding errors in the reading of dials and scales are not randomly distributed but, instead, are directed to one treatment condition rather than another, a systematic difference between treatments may emerge from the statistics. Subject effects may occur if the subject perceives the purpose of the experiment and seeks to cooperate too directly. Unwanted and invalid differences may also be introduced by instructions which affect performance over and above the planned distinctions between treatments. Some of these influences may even be communicated by gesture and other non-verbal cues.

Fortunately, remedies are at hand. A complicated but effective remedy in most situations is to dissociate the experimenter from the experimental designer. This ensures that the person who actually conducts the experiment and interacts with the subjects is ignorant of the purpose of the experiment. It is equally important that the purpose of the experiment should be unknown to whomsoever analyses the experimental data. This double or even triple 'blind' procedure helps a lot but does not provide perfect protection. It does not guard completely against systematic effects arising from the subjects' uninformed hypotheses about the nature of the experiment. It is also wise, therefore, to use only psychologically naive subjects.

It should be stressed that such complex empirical prophylaxis is unnecessary in experiments where there are powerful effects caused by the independent variables. These more subtle influences then may fade into the background. They are important, however, when the independent variable has a relatively weak influence or when the data can only be quantified by using human judgements. In general, given familiarity with the subject area and methodological sophistication, once a source of artefact has been identified a way of minimising its unwanted effects can be found.

Conclusions

This chapter has been devoted to a discussion of a number of issues concerning the nature of psychology and of psychological research. It has much in common with other sciences and the natural history of theories is of some interest. Psychology, perhaps because of its youth or because it has embraced relatively few researchers, is probably more subject to the whim of fashion than some other disciplines. The tendency for topics to be dropped rather than dealt with makes it sensible still to read classics such as William James's *Principles of Psychology* (1890).

The immutable nature of facts has been questioned, mainly on the grounds that it is not always obvious what counts as a fact. The ways in which theories can be tested has been examined. Finally, there has been some discussion of the vulnerability of data which may become distorted to fit into some theoretical preconception.

All of this is to show that adopting an empirical approach is no sure way to scientific salvation. However, sure or not it is the only road to follow. The road is tortuous and special skills are needed to avoid artefactual diversions. If we are to aspire eventually to understand the many and complex processes which underlie behaviour, there is no substitute for empirical research.

Further Reading

The other introductory and specialist volumes in this series are strongly recommended, particularly in the A section.

Annett, J. *Feedback and Human Behaviour.* (Harmondsworth: Penguin, 1969)

Bindra, D. and Stewart, J. (eds) *Motivation.* (Harmondsworth: Penguin, 1966)

Brit. Psych. Soc. *Psychology and Psychologists: a pamphlet for schools.* (London: Brit. Psych. Soc., 1970)

Brown, R. *Words and Things.* (Glencoe: Free Press, 1958)

Conant, J. B. *On Understanding Science.* (New Haven, Conn.: Yale Univ. Press, 1947)

Doll, R. and Hill, A. B. Mortality in relation to smoking: ten years' observations of British doctors. *Brit. Med. J., 1*: 1399–1460 (1964)

Fitts, P. and Posner, M. I. *Human Performance.* (Belmont, Cal.: Brooks/Cole, 1967)

Foss, B. M. (ed.) *Psychology in Great Britain.* (London: Brit. Psych. Soc., 1970)

Haber, R. N. (ed.) *Current Research in Motivation.* (New York: Holt, Rinehart and Winston, 1966)

Hall, C. S. *A Primer of Freudian Psychology.* (New York: New American Library, 1954)

Held, R. and Richards, W. (eds) *Perception: mechanisms and models.* (Readings from *Scientific American.*) (San Francisco and London: Freeman, 1972)

Herriot, P. *An Introduction to the Psychology of Language.* (London: Methuen, 1970)

Hill, W. F. *Learning: a survey of psychological interpretations.* (London: Methuen, 1964)

Holding, D. H. *Principles of Training.* (Oxford: Pergamon, 1965)

Hunter, I. M. L. *Memory, Facts and Fallacies.* (Harmondsworth: Penguin, 1957)

Jung, J. *Verbal Learning.* (New York: Holt, Rinehart and Winston, 1968)

Keele, S. W. *Attention and Human Performance.* (Pacific Palisades, Cal.: Goodyear, 1973)

Legge, D. (ed.) *Skills.* (Harmondsworth: Penguin, 1970)

Messick, D. M. (ed.) *Mathematical Thinking in Behavioural Sciences.* (Readings from *Scientific American.*) (San Francisco and London: Freeman, 1968)

Newcombe, T. (ed.) *New Directions in Psychology, I* (New York: Holt, Rinehart, Winston, 1962)

Newcombe, T. (ed.) *New Directions in Psychology, II* (New York: Holt, Rinehart, Winston, 1965)

Posner, M. I. *Cognition: an introduction* (Glenfield, Ill.: Scott, Foresman, 1973)

Reynolds, G. S. *A Primer of Operant Conditioning* (Glenfield, Ill.: Scott, Foresman, 1968)

Rosenthal, R. *Experimenter Effects in Behavioural Research* (New York: Appleton-Century-Crofts, 1966)

Ryle, G. *Concept of Mind* (Harmondsworth: Penguin, 1949)

Semeonoff, F. (ed.) *Personality Assessment* (Harmondsworth: Penguin, 1966)

Singleton, T. *Man-Machine Systems* (Harmondsworth: Penguin, 1974)

Thomson, R. *The Psychology of Thinking* (Harmondsworth: Penguin, 1959)

Wason, P. C. and Johnson-Laird, P. N. (eds.) *Thinking and Reasoning* (Harmondsworth: Penguin, 1968)

Weiner, N. *Cybernetics* (New York: Wiley, 1948)

References and Name Index

(The numbers in italics following each reference refer to page numbers within this book.)

Atkinson, R. C. and Shiffrin, R. M. (1967) Mathematical models for memory and learning. In D. P. Kimble (ed.) *Learning, Remembering and Forgetting, III*. New York: Academy of Sciences. *128*

Babbage, C. See Morrison, P. *17*

Broadbent, D. E. (1958) *Perception and Communication*. Oxford: Pergamon. *128*

Campbell, D. T. and Stanley, J. C. (1966) *Experimental and Quasi-experimental Designs for Research*. New York: Rand McNally. *38*

Chomsky, N. (1968) *Language and Mind*. New York: Harcourt, Brace and World. *97*

Eysenck, H. J. (1962) Smoking, personality and psychosomatic disorders. *J. Psychosom. Res.*, 7: 107–30. *37*

Eysenck, H. J. (1972) The experimental study of Freudian concepts. *Bull. Brit. Psychol. Soc.*, 25, (89): 261–7. *132*

Fechner, G. T. (1860) *Elemente der Psychophysik*. Leipzig: Breitkopf & Härtel. *60, 84*

Gall, F. J. and Spurzheim, G. (1810) *Anatomie et Physiologie du Système Nerveux*. Paris: Schoell. *16*

Galton, F. (1883) *Enquiries into Human Faculty and its Development*. London: Macmillan. *78*

Gregory, R. L. (1966) *Eye and Brain: the Psychology of Seeing*. New York: McGraw-Hill. *77*

Grey Walter, W. (1961) *The Living Brain*. Harmondsworth: Penguin. *103, 114*

Guthrie, E. R. (1935) *The Psychology of Learning*. New York: Harper. *54*

Hubel, D. H. and Wiesel, T. N. (1962) Receptive fields, binocular interaction and functional architecture in the cat's visual cortex. *J. Physiol. 160*: 106–54. *61*

Hull, C. L. (1951) *Essentials of Behaviour*. New Haven, Conn.: Yale University Press. *128*

James, W. (1890) *Principles of Psychology*. New York: Holt. *136*

Kintsch, W. (1970) *Learning, Memory and Conceptual Processes*. New York and London: Wiley. *35*

Lorenz, K. (1950) The comparative method in studying innate behaviour patterns. *Symposia of the Society for Experimental Biology 4*: 221–68. Cambridge University Press. *64*

Morrison, P. and Morrison, E. (eds) (1961) *Charles Babbage and his Calculating Engines*. New York: Dover Publications. *17*

Osgood, C. E. (1953) *Method and Theory in Experimental Psychology*. New York: Oxford University Press. *56*

Royal College of Physicians (1962) *Smoking in Relation to Cancer of the Lung and other Diseases*. London: R.C.P. *37*

Skinner, B. F. (1938) *The Behavior of Organisms*. New York: Appleton-Century. *117*

Spearman, C. (1927) *The Abilities of Man*. London: Macmillan. *38, 50*

Stevens, S. S. (ed.) (1951) *Handbook of Experimental Psychology*. New York: Wiley. *56*

Sutherland, N. S. (1964) Visual discrimination in animals. *Brit. Med. Bull. 20* (1): 54–9. *61*

Troland, L. T. (1928) *The Fundamentals of Human Motivation*. New York: Van Nostrand. *128*

Watson, J. B. (1919) *Psychology from the Standpoint of a Behaviourist*. Philadelphia: Lippincott. *12, 132*

Weber, E. H. (1846) Tastsinn und Gemeingefühl. In R. Wagner (ed.), *Handwörterbuch der Physiologie, III*: 481–588. *60, 84*

Whorf, B. L. (1956) *Language, Thought and Reality*. New York: Wiley. *98*

Woodworth, R. S. and Schlosberg, H. (1954) *Experimental Psychology*. London: Methuen. *56*

Wright, P., Hill, A. J. and Conrad, R. (1969) Performance tests with non-circular coins. *Ergonomics 12*: 1–10. *17*

Subject Index